'TWIXT THEE AND ME . . .

An Anthology
of Yorkshire and Lancashire
Verse and Prose

Companion Volumes : (edited by Joan Pomfret)

LANCASHIRE EVERGREENS
A hundred favourite old poems.

NOWT SO QUEER   (out of print)
SUMMAT FROM HOME (out of print)

'TWIXT THEE AND ME

An Anthology of

Yorkshire and Lancashire Verse and Prose

Selected and edited by

JOAN POMFRET

———————

1974
GERRARD PUBLICATIONS
6 Edge End Avenue,
BRIERFIELD, NELSON
Lancashire

JOHN HARRIS drew the cover picture. He used
an imaginary setting for the border stone.

ISBN Paperback edition 0 900397 26 8

ISBN Hardback edition 0 900397 25X

Printed by Turner & Earnshaw Ltd., Bread Street, Burnley

EDITOR'S NOTE

When Northcountry neighbours get together for a 'bit of a crack' the results are usually entertaining, sometimes surprising, and always enjoyable.

Here we have a collection of verse and prose from both sides of the Pennines - old and new, grave and gay, English and Dialect - a small hotchpotch of personal choice, like most anthologies, but with some attempt to show that ever since the days of Ben Preston and Edwin Waugh, Yorkshire and Lancashire writers have been inspired by similar things and have striven to express them in the same way.

The dialect items have been chosen from different corners of both counties, and thus present even wider spelling variations than usual. This does not make for easy reading, but, as I have always maintained, the only way to read dialect is to read it aloud. — I feel that the dialect-lover will readily take the trouble to 'translate', and the more serious student find interest in comparing, for example, poems like Arthur Jarratt's *'Innkeeper'* (Holderness, East Riding) with, say, Harvey Kershaw's *'Three Owd Maids'* (Rochdale, Lancashire).

To 'suit thisen' in Yorkshire, and to 'suit thisel' in Lancashire, mean exactly the same thing: i.e. to please yourself, do as you like, go your own way. The contributors to this miscellany have been doing this, just as I did in the book's compilation - we hope now that you, the reader, will also find something to 'suit thisen' (or thisel) in its pages.

Joan Pomfret

ACKNOWLEDGMENTS

The Publisher and Editor thank the under-mentioned for permission to reproduce certain items and extracts, namely:—

Borough of Accrington Library and Art Gallery Committee for *'Conversation'* and *'T' Band i' t' Park'* (from 'An Accrington Miscellany' 1970.)

Burnley Express, for *'The Wisest Dog in the World'* and *Lancashire English'*.

Mrs. G. O. Clayton, daughter of the late Dr. W. N. Pickles, for extracts from her father's personal diaries.

'Country Life', for the poem *'Tethered Astronauts'*.

'The Dalesman', for *'On Going Smokeless'*.

Hub Publications Ltd., for the two extracts from the plays *'Garlic Lane'* and *'Easy Street'* by John Waddington-Feather.

'Lancashire Life', for *'Collywobbles, Cucumber and Bumble Bees'* and *'Thilerman'*.

Lancashire Authors' Association Journal 'The Record' (Editor: R. Y. Digby) for various poems and stories.

Yorkshire Dialect Society's publications — ditto

'Yorkshire Ridings Magazine', for *'Haworth of the Brontës'*.

* * * * * *

The passage from *'South Riding'* is reproduced by kind permission of Winifred Holtby's literary executor, Mr. Paul Berry, and Curtis Brown Ltd.

The passage from *'Inheritance'* is reprinted by kind permission of A. D. Peters and Company, and of the author Phyllis Bentley.

Fred Brown's poems *'Light'* and *'The Little Piecer'* are taken with the author's permission from 'Songs of the Factory and the Loom', and 'More Songs of the Factory and the Loom'.

Walter Nugent Sinkinson's poem *'The Lost Train'* comes from his book 'Flying Scotsman and other Railway Poems'.

'In an Old Farm Kitchen' (Pavella D. Sutcliffe) was first printed in .\eflections', published by Preston Poets' Society in 1972.

* * * * * *

We also gratefully acknowledge the interest shown by the contributors themselves in the preparation of this book.

Our Lancashire authors rallied round as in our previous publications; they will not object if we mention the encouragement and practical help we received from the 'Yorkshire Side'! Authors, librarians, secretaries of organisations and friends co-operated whole-heartedly with our Lancashire editor, and it would be impossible, and indeed invidious, to mention them all individually.

But we are particularly grateful to Geoffrey Handley-Taylor for helpful advice, for the valuable information contained in his books *'Yorkshire Authors Today'* and *'Lancashire Authors Today'* (County Authors Today Series) — and most of all for allowing us to include his article *'Winifred Holtby and the Waste Paper Basket'*.

Special thanks are also due to Ian Dewhirst, Gwen Wade and other members of the Yorkshire Dialect Society, the Editor's first 'contacts' in Yorkshire.

CONTENTS (Yorkshire Section)

CONTENTS (Lancashire Section)

INTRODUCTION

We're apt to picture t'Pennine Way
As a dividing wall;
But when you come to think of it,
It's not like that at all.

Round here there's been an overspill,
The border bends and forks;
One minute you're in Lancashire,
The next step you're in Yorks.

We've lived here side by side for years
Without a lot of fuss;
We don't think there's a wall at all,
Or that there's 'Them' and 'Us'.

And though we know there's quite a gap
Between St. Annes and Hull,
And Manchester and Beverley
And Batley and Maghull —

That some folks think our counties still
Stand miles and miles apart;
What of it? Though we fratch a bit,
We're 'Varra like' at heart!

Yorkshire writers

THE FLITTING

Gwen Wade

THE last night in her own house, the house she had lived in ever since her marriage fifty years ago. Tomorrow she was to move into a room at The Sunset Home. *Sunset* indeed! Hadn't she been seeing sunsets back o' the fell all her life long?

Maggie had spent the best part of a year making up her mind to flit and had twice lost her place on the waiting-list, to the great annoyance of her family. To be fair to them, she had been a cause of anxiety, too. She did keep having these black-outs with little or no warning. There was the time when she hit her head on the dresser as she fell and had been forced to go into hospital for a while. And now her knees were so stiff that she couldn't get down to do her fireside or, if she got down, couldn't get up again for long enough. Yes, they were probably right, but then, *they* didn't have to leave their homes.

She had seen her new room. Maud had driven her down one day to meet the matron and some of the residents; all very pleasant, but old like herself. She preferred the company of young folk. The room was nice and she could have her own bits and pieces there, but – – – and there were two big buts,– – – there was only one of these electric fire-contraptions, and the house was down in the valley .. .. .. I've been a hill-top woman all my days – – – I'm used to hill-top ways and a breath of hill-top air. I'll feel smothered down there with the dark hillsides and only a peep of sky.!' .. .. There was a bell in the room which you could ring if you were in a fix, day or night, they said. But who was to ring the bell if she had a 'do' and fell? Best not to worrit about that, though, until the time came, if it ever did.

As she sat by her fire drinking a late cup of tea the thought came to her, 'I won't go to bed tonight, no, I won't. I'll sit here and enjoy a real fire for the last time, and take it all in so it's fresh in my mind. Besides that, t'bed won't need making in the morning. I'll not be miserable now, I'll think over all the good bits and t'rest I can leave behind me.'

A pang went through her at the memory of 't'rest' – – – the fact that none of her family would have her to live with them in her semi-invalid state. Her son Joe and his wife down in London

15

had cut themselves off from her long since, slammed the door in the face of the welfare officer who had tried to interview them about her. Em'ly? Well, Em'ly had her own troubles with that good-for-nothing man of hers. She had to go out to work when by rights at her age she should have been having things a bit easier. Em'ly, forty-six, and she still really thought of them all as bairns. She couldn't seem to realise that her family were all knocking on now, although it was small wonder with a mother of eighty-two, even if she *had* married rather late on.

Maud now, Maud could have taken her in. But Maud had grown posh – – – talked 'perlite' and you scarcely dared to sit yourself down in her best room for fear of disturbing something. Well, she'd not have been happy with Maud and her pernickety ways. Maud was forever pulling her up about her Yorkshire talk, but she wasn't going to scrape her tongue for anybody, not at her age, she wasn't. What was wrong with a bit of good Yorkshire talk anyway? 'Now then! Now then! No more o' these dowly thoughts! You're leaving them behind, think on!'

She rose with difficulty and made up her fire. Coal would just last out till the morning, she thought with satisfaction. Then she remembered the hills she was leaving and hobbled out to the door, supporting herself on the table edge as she passed. The night was clear and cold, with a high full moon which showed up the faint contour of the fells and lit the trunks of the two great sycamores which had served as a wind-break for the westerly gales. Maggie stood on her doorstep gazing at them. She wouldn't be able to keep the whole of them in her mind, not every twig of course, but she'd remember those horny old trunks all right and the sweep of the big branches and their shapes on the sky. Pity if she didn't, times she'd stood there waiting for one or other of them, or – – – just waiting for somebody who would never come again. Tears filled her eyes and she turned away to look at the moon. *That* old friend would come with her, choose how! Suddenly she chuckled out loud. A whisp of cloud had drawn a scowl across the moon's mouth. Maybe he was cross with her for loitering about out here and having gloomy thoughts. Yes, best go in, for it was cold – – – too cold.

After shutting the door she felt swimmy again and had to clutch the table for support. Better get sat down before she did anything daft. She lowered herself painfully into her fireside chair and sat for a few moments with her head low. She dozed off.

Waking suddenly, she said: 'I could have gone to *him* — — —
he'd have had me for sure.' She looked across at the dresser
where stood a photograph of a small smiling boy. 'Harry
wouldn't have let me go alone to a Sunset Home! *Born in sin*,
many of 'em said. But he wasn't, not that one. My sin ud have
been to let his dad go away without the comfort of my breast.
Canadian soldier, alone over here and nigh on desperate with
loneliness and his young wife dead back home. I wouldn't have
answered for what he might have done to himself if I hadn't
taken him in and given him my love. Grand lad, he was and
all — — — wrote to me a time or two after he'd gone back, but
gave up after I told him I'd got married. Only seemly really, and
me a deal older than him, too. I never told him about Harry. I
managed along and I didn't want him troubled. He'd enough on
his mind, had t'lad.

Then John came along and asked for me, and I told him fair
and square about Harry — — — he was living with mi Mam time I
was working. John was always good to him — — —treated him
fair even after his own bairns come. But there was me dreading
t'time when the rest would have to know they'd a different dad
from him. Then he took the fever at school. Eight year
old — — it's a long while since, but it seems like yesterday.
Forever laughing he was, and that kind to his mam, bless his
heart! Loved him best o' t' bunch, I did — — and lost him. Maybe
it was the happiest for him when all's said.'

Waking and dozing, now and then attending to her fire,
Maggie's memories travelled the years, pausing here and there
over an especial joy or sorrow, but not reaching up as far as her
husband's death which had come two years previously. Round
about four o'clock she began to feel cold and dizzy again, so
manoeuvred the kettle on to the fire to make herself some tea. It
was a struggle to get the teapot up again safely and she had to sit
awhile before gaining strength to pour it out. 'Yes, he'd have
cared for me, Harry would. He always used to say, "I'll be down
in the beck, Mam, but just give a holla if you want owt." He'd
have stayed that way — — it was his nature.'

Once more she began to feel dizzy, and there came that queer
red light she sometimes saw before the blackouts took her. She
straightened herself with an effort and saw the door open slowly.
'Why, Harry, bairn, has ta come for me?"

. . . .

17

When later in the morning Maud arrived to get her ready for the journey she thought that her mother had fallen asleep in her chair. She did not realise that the flitting was already accomplished.

NORTHENER

Dorothy Cowlin

I belong to the northlands.
Nothing extreme:
I pack no saga
or ice-axe in my bag —
but simply a land where the spring
comes halting,
ruminating on fronds of brown bracken
from last autumn;
harking back to December
with crescents of soiled snow;
where the light is the colour of grey eyes,
and the sun's warmth
filters through mists of white nylon;
where love and friendship
begin shyly but last well.
I could not endure to live
where the spring, however splendid,
burns out in two weeks, like a rocket.
February, the month of tentative promise,
is my birth-month.

JOHNNY LAD'S

Ian Dewhirst

The track still goes, as in other days,
By Johnny Lad's,
But Hiram's cows have the run of the place,
And Ezra's sheep,
And it seems, in lee of the streaming hills,
To be drowning in mud to the very sills
(And the farmer has long lain buried deep,
Of Johnny Lad's.)

Now nettles crowd in the mildew rooms
Of Johnny Lad's,
On sinks and larders as cold as tombs,
On grates ne'er light,
While magpies flap with their chatter-cry
Where the crazy stairs climb up to the sky
(For the tired slates drop in the night
From Johnny Lad's.)

And a tree bears strange fruits
At Johnny Lad's,
Growing bent from its nibbled roots
In the empty air,
For the bottle-green harness hung in the crook
Will never be ripe with the August shook
(And what of the man who swung it there
At Johnny Lad's?)

There are relics still of the life they made
At Johnny Lad's,
For bits of books still hug the shade
On the drier side,
And Hiram's cows still turn them up—
(A rusty shovel, the half of a cup)
(But the children are old and far and wide,
From Johnny Lad's.)

LIZZ LECKONBY'S 'LECTRIC BLANKET

J. Fairfax-Blakeborough

OLD Lizzie Leckonby's favourite niece (the one who most of us expect will 'come in for what Lizzie has, when the time comes') has given her aunt an electric-blanket. We have known for some time that one or two people in the village have these winter comforts, but generally speaking they are considered daring, venturesome and a suspect mystery.

When she received the present Lizzie Leckonby was not grateful and quite decided that she would never use it. However, when her niece showed her how simple it was to 'plug in' and disconnect, and how it warmed her aunt's bed far better than her brass warming-pan, followed by a hot water-bottle at the top and a heated brick 'lapped in flannil' at the foot, Lizzie became a convert. She has since never tired of telling her visitors of the simplicity, warmth and comfort the 'lectric blanket gives when she had 'satten t'fire out and gans ti bed niddered with cawd.'

There has been so much talk, curiosity, wonderment and inspection of Lizzie's electric blanket that it is not surprising that it should be discussed at the weekly sewing-meeting, which is the receiving and clearing house of all the gossip of the parish.

Mrs. Mary Thompson was the first to introduce the subject. Either Mary is full of jealousy, or full of suspicious fear (or both) for she began: "We've all heeard of a certain party, what's so far forgotten the position the Lord has called her to occipy, as ti hape and himitate her betters, and be different to other folks by getting summat which she doesn't understand, and which may onny night hend in her being hurried inti eternity a roasted corpse. What's more, and this is where I (what has the misfotten ti live next door) and hother nybors comes in. We all stands in danger of having our homes bont down over our heads, and be 'lectrocuted as frazzled hashes intiv kingdom come. There owt ti be a law again sike higgerant, hinsufficient, hancient, himcompetent awd women being 'lowed on ti harbour sike-like dangerous hinventions. They're warse nor these nuclear bumbs yan hears so mich about, and they're nowt but hupstarts, show-off, vanity, which no-one knows orther the beginning or hend of.

"She's on about mi 'lectric blanket what my niece sent me," exclaimed Lizzie Leckonby, who went on: "It's comed tiv a bonny pass if I has ti hask Mary Thompson's permission ti use summat what I owns up I wad nivver have thowt of buying, but which I wadn't be without now, nut was it hever so!"

"I was delighted to hear you had got such a useful present, now that the cold nights have come," said the vicar's wife. "We had a present made of an electric blanket, and find it a great comfort. When we have guests staying at the Vicarage I always put it in their bed, and then we find out how much better it is than hot-water bottles. Of course, electric-blankets have to be used with great care. I wouldn't like to leave the Vicarage when ours is in a bed with the current on, and I wouldn't like anyone in the house to go to sleep before switching off the current."

"That's the very pint!" broke in Mary Thompson. "Sike new-fangled 'lectric hinventions should honly be selled to and used by them what unnerstands about vollts, currents, positives and negatives and that, and what's tutored up in 'Lectricity. Folks what goes in for sike like wants all their wits about 'em, and be in possession of all the faculties, and nut be reggler nodders off ti sleep like Elizabeth Leckonby is. Nobody can say that, in a way o' speaking, Elizabeth knows the fosst thing about the dangerous thing she brags about. An helectric blanket in her hands is a menace, a danger, and a threat to the life and property of the wole village. I knows what it'll end in — a conflagration; all on us bont tiv a cinder and 'lectrocuted in our sleep, with the chetch and chappil i' ruins. Unless Lizzie Leckonby can be stopped in her vanity, vetersome folly and tempting of the Halmighty to hutterly destroy and wipe oot this village, we're hall on the hedge of a hay-biss, which no one can say when the volcano will busst. I'm going ti mak it my business ti see fother inti it when the 'lectricity man comes round next."

Rachel Raby next aired her views. She said: "Lizzie showed me the contraption which looked innercent enough, but I telled her she didn't know what she was letting of hersen in for. She knows no mair about 'lectricity nor what I does — and that's nowt! 'Lectricity's nut a thing ti be played with. You might as well give a hinfant in arms a razor and expect nowt ti happen, as give Elizabeth a thing she's not heddicated up to. I can't give her no comfort. She's takking a dangerous viper inti bed with her, and sooner or later she'll be bit, and mebbe come tiv a bad end.

I've read in the papers about sike like happenings, and, as it says in the scripters, Lizzie and them what live high-hand will sleep i' jeopardy every night so long as that thing thrussen full of 'lectricity is on the go. You know anybody wad be dropped on ti wakken up and finnd theirselves 'lectrocuted, or roasted corpses!"

"Of course these blankets have to be used with care and examined from time to time," said the vicar's wife. "But they are not so dangerous as Miss Raby seems to think. Thousands of people use them, and we only hear of the rare cases of an accident with one."

"Its mebbe less ventersome for them what has brains and unnerstands what's what, and ti what things belongs, ti put them things in their beds. If owt goes wrang they'll have some gumption what ti do, and what's mair, they'll nut tummel off ti sleep with the thing gitting hotter and hotter. Nobody can say that Lizzie Leckonby has orther the brains nor the hexperience. I'm nut thinking so mich of her being frazzled up and bot tive a cinder as the fire she starts spreading ti folks what lives close by, and what knows their positions better than ti try ti himmitate quality folk."

"I taks no more notish ti Mary Thompson's himpident hinsults tharr I does to the twittering of birds!" retorted Lizzie Leckonby. "I finnds the blanket a great comfort. I've been showed the way ti gan on wiv it, and I've no call ti ask horther Mary Thompson's advice nor her permission orther as ti when I tons it on, or tons it hoff, so I think we'll change the subjeck and talk aboot summat helse."

WINTER AT LOWOOD

Charlotte Brontë (1816 – 1855)

DURING January, February, and part of March, the deep snows, and, after their melting, the almost impassable roads, prevented our stirring beyond the garden walls, except to go to church, but within these limits we had to pass an hour every day in the open air. Our clothing was insufficient to protect us from the severe cold; we had no boots, the snow got into our shoes, and melted there; our ungloved hands became numbed and covered with chilblains, as were our feet. I remember well the distracting irritation I endured from this cause every evening, when my feet inflamed, and the torture of thrusting the swelled, raw and stiff toes into my shoes in the morning. Then the scanty supply of food was distressing: with the keen appetites of growing children, we had scarcely sufficient to keep alive a delicate invalid. From this deficiency of nourishment resulted an abuse which pressed hardly on the younger pupils: whenever the famished great girls had an opportunity they would coax or menace the little ones out of their portion. Many a time I have shared between two claimants the precious morsel of brown bread distributed at tea-time, and after relinquishing to a third half the contents of my mug of coffee, I have swallowed the remainder with an accompaniment of secret tears, forced from me by the exigency of my hunger.

Sundays were dreary days in that wintry season. We had to walk two miles to Brocklebridge Church, where our patron officiated. We set out cold, we arrived at church colder: during the morning service we became almost paralysed. It was too far to return to dinner, and an allowance of cold meat and bread, in the same penurious proportion observed in our ordinary meals, was served round between the services.

At the close of the afternoon service we returned by an exposed and hilly road, where the bitter wind, blowing over a range of snowy summits to the north, almost flayed the skin from our faces. I can remember Miss Temple walking lightly and rapidly along our drooping line, her plaid cloak, which the frosty wind fluttered, gathered close about her, and encouraging us, by precept and example, to keep up our spirits, and march forward, as she said, "like stalwart soldiers." The other teachers, poor things, were generally themselves too much dejected to attempt the chance of cheering others.

How we longed for the light and heat of a blazing fire when we got back! But, to the little ones at least, this was denied; each hearth in the schoolroom was immediately surrounded by a double row of great girls and behind them the younger children crouched in groups, wrapping their starved arms in their pinafores.

A little solace came at tea-time, in the shape of a double ration of bread – a whole, instead of a half, slice – with the delicious addition of a thin scrape of butter; it was the hebdomadal treat to which we all looked forward from Sabbath to Sabbath. I generally contrived to reserve a moiety of this bounteous repast for myself: but the remainder I was invariably obliged to part with.

The Sunday evening was spent in repeating, by heart, the Church Catechism, and the fifth, sixth, and seventh chapters of St. Matthew; and in listening to a long sermon, read by Miss Miller, whose irrepressible yawns attested her weariness. A frequent interlude of these performances was the enactment of the part of Eutychus by some half-dozen of little girls: who, overpowered with sleep, would fall down, if not out of the third loft, yet off the fourth form, and be taken up half dead. The remedy was, to thrust them forward into the centre of the schoolroom, and oblige them to stand there till the sermon was finished. Sometimes their feet failed them, and they sank together in a heap; they were then propped up with the monitors' high stools.

COUNTRY STATION

Gordon Allen North

We nubbut stopped a minute
                    theer —
  't wor nowt mich 'n a spot —
a tooathri haases raand a
                    choch,
    a schooil, a vacant lot,
a pub 'at leeaned druff 'nly
    ageean a stumpy yew,
a duck pond in a mucky
                    yard,
    a stack or two.

But t'bods wor theer, an'
    t'sun wor theer,
an' t'trees wor varry green;
    wol up aboon, wor t'
                    bluest sky
'at yo'n ivver seen.
A whistle skriked, we pooled
                    away.
an' t'Diesel's dizzy
                    din.
reminded me o' t'bletherin'
    o' monny a comer-in.

YORK'S OLD STAINED GLASS

A. L. Laishley

IN YORK there is the largest assembly in the country of ancient stained and painted glass; in fact it is estimated that the city has half of all the old glass in England. Almost all of it is in the Minster and the city churches.

Of the Minster's 126 windows three are particularly outstanding, not only because of the quality of their glass and their great age but also of their very size. In order of age these are the Five Sisters (13th century), Great West (14th century) and the Great East (15th century). The 700 year-old Five Sisters Window in the North Transept is made up of five lancets, each of which is over 50ft. long and 5ft. wide. How it got its name is not really known except that Charles Dickens wrote a fictitious story about its origin in *Nicholas Nickleby*. When Nicholas and Squeers, the schoolmaster bully, were journeying north from London to Dotheboys Hall, their coach broke down, and to while away the time until it was repaired, the travellers entertained one another by each telling a story – there being no television for them to watch! One old man told how five sisters who lived in York occupied their time in working lengths of tapestry. When the youngest sister died the remaining four had their needlework copied in stained glass as a memorial to her. A moving story, but unfortunately with no record to prove its truth. Dickens is known to have visited York at intervals to see his brother Alfred who was employed by the 'new' railway company.

He knew the Minster well, and no doubt the very nature of the window's 13th. century grisaille glass fired his fertile imagination to produce the five sisters and their needlework, for the coloured geometric patterns super-imposed on a grey-green background certainly give the impression of tapestry. Some people think this window dull, but get the correct light upon it and you will see that the patterns include little sparkling jewels of brightly coloured glass.

When it was due to be replaced in the 1920s after having been removed for safety prior to the 1914-18 War it was badly in need of releading – for it is strips of lead which hold the glass together in a stained glass window – and there are over 100,000 tiny pieces of glass in this window. Lead lasts no longer than 120 years; after that the window must be releaded if the window is to remain intact. For a window of this size tons of lead are needed. How was it ever to be acquired? The incredible story is that sufficient lead of a date contemporary with the window itself was found at Rievaulx Abbey in North Yorkshire. At that time Sir Charles Peers was excavating there when he came across several ingots of lead buried in the ground; the lead had been there since 1539 when the abbey was Dissolved, for it was still stamped with Henry V111's Seal. One of the first jobs of the King's men when a monastery was about to be closed was to strip the lead from the roof, for it was valuable, and Henry was always in need of money. We shall never know whether these ingots found in 1924 had been overlooked, or whether the monks had deliberately buried them, hoping to recover them at a later date. It was this lead which was used to relead York Minster's five giant windows in the North Transept — one can only hope that the monks would have approved.

The Great West Window, over 54ft. by 25ft., which is above the Great West Door, is best seen in the late afternoon of a summer's day when, with a background of golden evening light, it literally glows with colour. The Very Rev. Eric Milner-White whose life between the years 1941 and 1963 when he died, was devoted to the extensive restoration of the Minster's priceless glass, used to say the glaziers 'painted on light', and this is never better seen than when the Great West Window is backed by the evening sun. The window was given by Archbishop Melton in the year 1338 and cost a hundred Marks (about £67). His badge, a trefoil leaf, can be seen in both tracery and borders. The panels include a number of former Archbishops of York, including the donor, and several Apostles, while the topmost panels are devoted to scenes from the life of Our Lord and the Virgin Mary. After the 1914-18 War the City of Bradford generously contributed to its restoration; after the 1939-45 War its return in 1967 signified the completion of over 20 years work on the Minster's glass. In the Nave there is the finest collection of 14th. century stained glass in the world; each window has its own beauty and character, but the finest of all is the window in the centre of the west wall.

The Great East Window covers the area of a tennis court. It was created by John Thornton of Coventry between the years

1405 and 1408, and his initials can be seen at the window's apex. After its last restoration, which took 11 years to complete, one glazier completing one 3ft-square panel in one month, Dr. Milner-White added his initials as well. He used to say, with a twinkle, how he 'climbed up to the apex ably supported by the Clerk of Works' and scratched his initials in the approved manner, with a diamond. The theme of the window is The Beginning and the End. In the apex God the Father is seen with an open book in front of Him on which are the words, 'Ego Sum Alpha et Omega' (I am the Beginning and the End). He is surrounded in the tracery by the Company of Heaven. Below, the first three rows of panels are devoted to Old Testament pictures from the Creation to the Death of Absalom; the rest (except for the last few panels which portray kings) to the End as seen by St. John the Divine in the Book of Revelations. Most of the windows in the eastern arm of the Minster are contemporary with the early 15th. century architecture. Among them in the choir transepts are the huge St. William window (to the north) and the St. Cuthbert window (to the south); each tells the story of the respective saint's life and miracles.

About 80 of the Minster's windows were removed for safety at the beginning of the 1939-45 War. Then began a mighty restoration in which each window was cleaned, restored, releaded and eventually replaced. Glass that was foreign to the windows but which had been added during former releadings to replace broken glass was replaced by suitable pieces from the 'glass banks' in the glaziers' shop, and the panels worked jig-saw wise to restore them as nearly as possible to their original patterns of Biblical stories in stained glass. Over the centuries strange mistakes had been made, perhaps the most amusing (in the Great East Window) one that had given Noah a brown cow as a hat. I need hardly say that the cow was restored to the Ark, and Noah supplied with a more fitting headgear. If you look through a pair of opera glasses or binoculars (and that is the most satisfactory way to study these enormous windows) you will see that the cow now looks contentedly through a window in the Ark.

Of the glass in the York churches the most famous is that in All Saints', North Street. Two outstanding windows are in the north aisle, one depicting the last fifteen days of the world, as described in an old poem called The Pryke of Conscience. This window should be 'read' in rows, from the left, beginning at the bottom. It includes such scenes as the waters rising and then receding, the stars falling, sea monsters issuing from the water, the dead rising from their graves, ... Less horrifying is the neighbouring window, the six corporal acts of mercy as recounted by St. Matthew — the feeding of the hungry, giving drink to the thirsty, visiting the sick and those in prison, welcoming the stranger, clothing the naked. The burial of the dead, the 7th. act of mercy, is omitted.

The great east window in this church is a gem of 15th. century glass with, in the central light, St. Anne teaching her daughter, the Child Virgin, to read, while in the south aisle is a colourful window showing the Nine Orders of Angels — one figure is unique in that he is wearing spectacles. Good 14th. century glass is at the east of the north aisle — glass with that rich golden hue which first appeared in the 14th. century, being discovered by accident when a workman's sleeve smeared with silver chloride glass which was about to be fired in a kiln. The smeared portion came out yellow, and so a new process was born.

Another church whose 31ft. window of 15th. century glass is a 'must' for stained glass lovers who come to York is the St. Martin window in the Church of St. Martin-le-Grand, Coney Street. This 15th. century church was almost wholly destroyed in an air-raid in 1942, but the south aisle, the former Lady Chapel, has been rebuilt, old features being incorporated with new, resulting in a little 'new-old' church of rare beauty. Fortunately the former great west window was taken out in 1939 and it is now in a specially built five-sided tower in the north wall. It shows scenes from the life of the patron saint, Martin of Tours. In contrast, the east window in this church is modern, one of abstract design by Harry Stammers. It depicts the flames which destroyed the 15th. century church, and beyond the red of the flames the colours fade gradually into a pearly-white to give an impression of the peace of the next life after the turmoil of this world. Harry Stammers' work may also be seen in the Church of St. Olave (reached through the Museum Gardens) in a little window of a very different style. Here the subject is the Annunciation and shows the Virgin and the Angel in Stammers' very distinctive style.

Fourteenth century windows showing the Passion of Our Lord are in the Church of All Saints, Pavement; a fine 15th. century 5-light window in Holy Trinity Church, Goodramgate, with the central light depicting the Holy Trinity — a full-length figure of the Wounded Christ with the Holy Dove above His Head, and God the Father appearing over His left shoulder. There is good 16th. century glass (a time when the art was not at its best) in St. Michael-le-Belfrey Church near the Minster, including St. George killing a lurid red dragon; enamel glass of the 18th. century, by the York glass-painter William Peckitt, in St. Martin-cum-Gregory Church, Micklegate; and a fine east window of heavy Victorian glass in St. Helen's Church, St. Helen's Square, the subject the Four Evangelists and their Emblems the Angel-man, Lion, Ox, and the Eagle. A small panel showing the glasspainters' arms is also here, in the east window of the south aisle, for St. Helen's was the Guild Church of the medieval glasspainters who mostly lived in Stonegate nearby. It is the work of Henry Gyles, the 17th. century York glasspainter.

LIGHT

Fred Brown

Give us some leet
The weyver said,
As he cupped his hands
And held his head;
Give us some leet
An' then ah can see
To daahn mi piece in t'morning:

Haa much leet,
The maister sed,
Haah much leet
For a sleepy yed?
Tha mun rub thi een
An' then tha'll see
To daahn thi piece in t'morning:

A hawporth o' leet
The weyver said,
A tallow wick
To addle mi bread;
Ther'll be leet enough
For thee to see,
When tha perches mi piece in t'morning.

A VISIT TO HAWORTH PARSONAGE

(From a letter quoted by Mrs. Gaskell in her 'Life of Charlotte Brontë.')

"It must have been about this time that a visit was paid to her (Charlotte) by some neighbours, who were introduced to her by a mutual friend. This visit has been described in a letter from which I am permitted to give extracts, which will show the impression made upon strangers by the character of the country round her home and other circumstances. . ."

T HOUGH the weather was drizzly, we resolved to make our long-planned excursion to Haworth; so we packed ourselves into the buffalo-skin, and that into the gig, and set off about eleven. The rain ceased, and the day was just suited to the scenery — wild and chill — with great masses of cloud glooming over the moors, and here and there a ray of sunshine covertly stealing through, and resting with a dim magical light upon some high bleak village; or darting down into some deep glen, lighting up the tall chimney or glistening on the windows and wet roof of the mill which lies couching in the bottom. The country got wilder and wilder as we approached Haworth; for the last four miles we were ascending a huge moor, at the very top of which lies the dreary black-looking village of Haworth. The village street itself is one of the steepest hills I have ever seen, and the stones are so horribly jolting that I should have got out and walked with W - - - if possible, but having once begun the ascent, to stop was out of the question. At the top was the inn where we put up, close by the church; and the clergyman's house, we were told, was at the top of the churchyard. So through that we went — a dreary, dreary place, literally *paved* with rain-blackened tomb-stones, and all on the slope, for at Haworth there is on the highest height a higher still, and Mr. Brontë's house stands considerably above the church. There was the house before us, a small, oblong stone house, with not a tree to screen it from the cutting wind; but how were we to get at it from the churchyard we could not see. There was an old man in the churchyard, brooding like a Ghoul over the graves, with a sort of grim hilarity on his face. I thought he looked hardly human; however, he was human enough to tell us the way; and presently we found ourselves in the little bare parlour. Presently the door opened, and in came a superannuated mastiff, followed by an old gentleman very like Miss Brontë, who shook hands with us, and then went to call his daughter. A long interval, during which we coaxed the old dog, and looked at a picture of Miss Brontë, by Richmond, the solitary ornament of the room, looking strangly out of place on the bare walls, and at the books on the little shelves, most of them evidently the gifts of the authors since Miss Brontë's celebrity. Presently she came in, and welcomed us very kindly, and took me upstairs to take off my bonnet, and herself brought me water and towels. The uncarpeted stone stairs and floors, the old drawers propped on wood, were all scrupulously clean and neat. When we went into the parlour again, we began talking very comfortably, when the door opened and Mr.Brontë looked in; seeing his daughter there, I suppose he thought it was all right, and he retreated to his study on the opposite side of the passage; presently emerging again to bring W--- a country newspaper. This was his last appearance till we went. Miss Brontë spoke with the greatest warmth of Miss Martineau, and of the good she had gained from her. Well! we talked about various things; the character of the people – about her solitude etc., till she left the room to help about dinner, I suppose, for she did not return for an age. The old dog had vanished; a fat curly-haired dog honoured us with his company for some time, but finally manifested a wish to get out, so we were left alone. At last she returned, followed by the maid and dinner, which made us all more comfortable; and we had some very pleasant conversation, in the midst of which time passed quicker than we supposed, for at last W--- found that it was half-past three, and we had fourteen or fifteen miles before us. So we hurried off, having obtained from her a promise to pay us a visit in the spring; and the old gentleman having issued once more from his study to say goodbye, we returned to the inn, and made the best of our way homewards.

Miss Brontë put me so in mind of her own 'Jane Eyre'. She looked smaller than ever, and moved about so quietly and noiselessly, just like a little bird, as Rochester called her, barring that all birds are joyous, and that joy can never have entered that house since it was first built; and yet, perhaps, when that old man married, and took home his bride, and children's voices and feet were heard about the house, even that desolate crowded graveyard and biting blast could not quench cheerfulness and hope. Now there is something touching in the sight of that little creature entombed in such a place, and moving about herself like a spirit, especially when you think that the slight still frame encloses a force of strong fiery life, which nothing has been able to freeze or extinguish."

MRS. DICK

Gwen Wade

FATHER! Father! theer's t'telegraph lass — whativver's amiss, nah? It'll be be mi Auntie Meg, Ah sudn't wunner, an mi best costume's at t'cleaners an all! . . . Eh? . . .Wot? . . . Nay, ther's no answer, lass . . . Nay, it's not bad news, thankin thee all t'seam . . . . . Nah be off oam tha nosey little monkey, it's no business o' thine!

Father! Father! Tha'll nivver credit it, nivver in t'wo'ld — ahr Dick's gettn hissen wed tiv a Lunnon lass and he's fotchin her oam toneet . . . Ahr Dick wed! An tiv a Lunnon lass — well, if that doesn't cap all! Why, it *says* he's wed! Here, Ah'll read it aht to thee, tha'll be all o' twenty minute laitin efter thi glasses an fassenin them on thi nose . . . . "Married Mary Maine in London Tuesday, bringin her oam toneet .— *night* — Dick."

Father! They'll be landin wi t'seven bus an mi beakin's not aht o' t'oven yet an all them sheets hauf dry on t'line an t'best bedstead's caster's broke an young Rover's lugged best part o' t'feathers aht o' t'bed an ther's a mahse gone an nested in t'oil! Lord a mercy, what's t'lad thinkin abaht!

Father! Ah'll lay onny money shoo's a lady an shoo'll talk Lunnon an wear them minis an whativver shall Ah call her by? Ah cannut say . . . Miss Mary, nor yet . . .Miss Maine, cos it wearn't sahnd menseful along of her bein wed, an if Ah says *Mrs. Dixon.* it'll be lahk clackin wi missen, an *Mrs. Dick* sahnds war. But Ah couldn't nivver bring misen ti say *Mary* tiv her; why it'd sahnd reight cheeky, sam as if Ah said *George* to t'passon! . . . Eh deary me, whativver. . . .

Oh ay, laff! It's eppen nowt to thee at thy onny son's getten hissen wed tiv a city piece at wearn't demean hersen wi t'weshin an cleanin an cahrs aht all o' t'dea in t'rockin' chair wetchin her awd mother-in-law tewin her fingers to t'boan. . .

Why nah, whoivver's clankin t'geate at this tahm o' t'dea an me wi tea ti set on an all! FATHER! It's them! They've landed!
. . . . .

Why Dick, lad, it's grand to clap een on thee wed *or* single, but wheer's — ? Flayed to come in? A Lunnon lass flayed! . . . Shoo's nivver hed noa folk sin---? Fotch her in, Dick? It's nawther mense ner sense leavin thi bride starvin on t' doorstun... They carried em ower i mah young deas, *didn't they, Father?*

Come your weays in Miss----Missis----Oh lawks, Ah'm that stagnated Ah doan't reetly knaw what Ah'm sayin! Come on in, luv, an let's hev a lewk at yer... Ah tellt thee, Father, Ah'd nivver call her *Mary*, not iv a month o' Sundas.... What, lass? Ye've hed noa mother to call thee *Mary* this fifteen year? Why then, if it's to be *Mary* fro me, it'll need to be *Mother* fra thee.... An this is Father, lass. His bark's war ner his bite an he moastly onny barks at W.I.neets when his supper's a bit leate on t' table.

A grand smell o' beakin? Lawks, them cheese ceaks'll be cotchin, if ye'll excuse me a minute... Ay, it *is* a grand oven is this... So you was cook in t'WAF!.. Nah, nah, if that inn't a co-in-side-ance---ahr Annie wor in t'WAF an all!.. Nay, lass, we lost her. They machine-gunned t'station — her commander tellt us shoo mad a wonderful end — Ah'll shew thee t' letter one o' these deas .... Lawks! If it inn't rainin fit ti drahn t'ark an them sheets is aht yet! .... Tha'll fotch em in whal Ah gets t'pastries aht? Bless thee, luv, it'll be grand ti eve another pair o'hands on t'spot — t'menfolk was born wi'aht em seeminly!

Dick! Get on aht an help thi missis, tha'll finnd t'voider in t'back kitchin, an Ah'll eve tea on t'table i two wags o' Rover's tail. Father! Leet t'fire in t'best bedroom and set them blankets an sheets on t'rail ti be airin'; it'll nivver do ti get her wi brahnchitis t'fost neet shoo lands oam...

Why nah, lass, that's reet kind on yer. Come in an get weshed an we'll sit dahn tiwer teas----ther's nowt knocks t'stuffin aht on yer lahk gettin wed, tha knaws.

What, Father? Wheer'st' kindlin? Why in t' stick-oil o' course, gormless! What a man! How*ivver* Ah've run this farm baht a woman's help, Ah doan't knaw! Eh, Mary Luv, it'll be reet champion wi a dowter in t'owd spot!

THE BROOKSIDE

Richard Monckton Milnes (Lord Houghton)
1809-1885.

I wandered by the brook-side,
I wandered by the mill,---
I could not hear the brook flow,
The noisy wheel was still;
There was no burr of grasshopper,
Nor chirp or any bird,
But the beating of my own heart
Was all the sound I heard.

I sat beneath the elm-tree,
I watched the long, long shade,
And as it grew still longer,
I did not feel afraid;
For I listened for a footfall,
I listened for a word,---
But the beating of my own heart
Was all the sound I heard.

He came not, ---no, he came not,---
The night came on alone,---
The little stars sat, one by one,
Each on his golden throne;
The evening air passed by my cheek,
The leaves above were stirr'd,---
But the beating of my own heart
Was all the sound I heard.

Fast, silent, tears were flowing,
When something stood behind,
A hand was on my shoulder,
I knew its touch was kind:
It drew me nearer---nearer,---
We did not speak one word,
For the beating of our own hearts
Was all the sound we heard.

CHARLES FORSHAW:
THE GREAT ANTHOLOGIST

Stephen Wade

C HARLES Forshaw is remembered by few Yorkshire people today, and those who are familiar with his writings will know him as an anthologist of Yorkshire poetry rather than as a poet. He was a dental surgeon in professional life at Bradford, but the love of poetry and local history in him led to the production of a vast amount of literature on Yorkshire and Yorkshire writers.

Forshaw was born in Bilsdon, Staffs, on January 23rd, 1863. He studied chemistry and dentistry, and became a doctor of Dental Surgery in 1885. During his time as a dentist he received many honours, including an honorary LL.D. from Tusculum University, Tennessee, and an M.D. from Chicago. National Medical University. He also wrote papers on the use of cocaine and on the microscopic structure of teeth. His early biographer, J.G. Gibson, collected all the facts about the honours conferred on Forshaw, and the statistics of his literary career. Gibson says that "He has today (1908) written over one thousand biographies of poets and poetasters. . . fifty publications have issued from his pen. . . he has contributed verses to more than 5,000 journals and newspapers."

What Forshaw did have was an unusual bent for producing anthologies. He edited sixteen collections of poetry of various kinds, mostly occasional poems or Yorkshire poetry. His love for the collection of a wide assortment of poems on a set theme for instance, was constantly with him throughout his career. He collected anthologies of monodies on the deaths of Queen Victoria, W. E. Gladstone, Sir Henry Irving, and others. In the lists of his publications there are also such collections as "One hundred of the best poems on the European War, by poets of the Empire", and "Poetical tributes on the loss of the R.M.S. 'Titanic'."

Forshaw's writings, or collections of other people's writings, are prodigious in number; yet, of all his interests in poetry, there is one sphere in which his work will always be useful to the student, and that is Yorkshire literature. In his lecture "Some Yorkshire poets" (1910), a poetry recital interspersed with a few biographical remarks, he gives some account of his work as an anthologist of Yorkshire writing :—

"In the course of issuing my collections of Yorkshire poetry I have come across upwards of two thousand Yorkshiremen who have written poetry ... I have known of the millionaire Yorkshire poet — only one instance though — and I have known of poets who have died in workhouses and prisons — all Yorkshiremen, bear in mind. . . four of them were appointed Poet Laureate."

Above all else, Forshaw was an antiquary, a compulsive collector, but his importance does not end there. He did produce some work of literary value, and although he published half a dozen books of poetry of his own, the works that are of value are his prose writings. His lecture, mentioned above, is a valuable source-book for anyone interested in Victorian literature, but his best work is in "John Hartley: Poet and Author", and in his collections of Yorkshire poets with introductions in "Poets of Keighley, Bingley and Haworth" (1891), which includes examples of the work of John Nicholson the Airedale poet, and of Patrick Brontë.

In his essay on John Hartley, the well-known founder of the "Clock Almanac" and author of the "Yorkshire Ditties", there are fine passages of lively prose; as, for instance, in this account of Hartley giving a lecture in Quebec:—

"The streets became rivers and traffic was stopped. One solitary individual managed to reach the hall in some way, and our Hartley waited patiently but in vain for an audience, but no-one appeared! He was not to be deterred, however, and punctually made his appearance on the platform and went through the hour and a half entertainment to his audience of ONE!"

This work on Hartley is brief, but it discloses the character of the dialect poet perfectly. At the end of the essay there is a subscription list applying for a Civil List Pension for Hartley, which includes the names of people famous in literary history, like Joseph Wright the Anglo-Saxon scholar, and W.S. Baring-Gould, the author of "Onward Christian Soldiers", and curate of Horbury near Wakefield. Forshaw himself subscribed of course, and the warmth of his essay on Hartley suggests that the wealthy Bradford dentist probably used all his influence to help Hartley in his old age.

Throughout his literary career, Forshaw went on writing poems and compiling anthologies, and it seems a little sad that today his efforts have been forgotten by all but the keen students of Yorkshire history and literature. Yet in his own day he was immensely successful, becoming a Fellow of the Royal Society of Literature and a Fellow of the Royal Historical Society. He was also a founder-member of the Brontë Society and the Thoresby Society.

All accounts of him suggest a really full life, with even a touch of romance; much of his spare time was spent in giving lectures, editing anthologies and journals such as "Yorkshire Notes and Queries", but there were times when he entered an entirely different world. In the Coronation year of Edward VII, for instance, Forshaw was made "King's Messenger" and chosen to deliver a message from the king to the people of St.Kilda. Naturally when he returned, out came pen and paper, and he produced a history of St. Kilda — "for the young princes" he said.

An even more incongruous event took place in 1904: for he was made, of all things, a Welsh Bard in that year! Forshaw was given the name of Siarl Efrog, which means "Charles of York", and, as if this honour was not enough, he became Chevalier of the Order of Duty, France, as well.

Who else could claim the title of true Yorkshireman more confidently than this character? It seems strange that a man with so many academic honours did not produce a major work of criticism, but his work in Yorkshire certainly brought Forshaw fame in his lifetime. He wished to be recognised above all as a poet, and he kept on writing poetry, but alas, it has little worth and is forgotten. What could be more uninspired than:—

> "Ye confused coronets of celebrated grace
> That brightly gilt the arching dome of Heaven"

in his poem "To the Stars"? Or, in his poem to "The London Fog", the lines:—

> "Men more like goblins, ghastly, gaunt and grim,
> Enshrouded and enveloped 'mid its maze."?

Few people will find satisfaction in these thoughts today. Nevertheless, Forshaw clearly enjoyed his writing, and saw fit to collect anthologies of Yorkshire verse. The thing that must surely puzzle his readers is the fact that he never wrote verse in the Yorkshire dialect. He admired the dialect as a medium for homely Yorkshire philosophy, and also became acquainted with the dialect poets, Ben Turner, Hartley and Edwin Waugh during his lifetime. It remains a mystery. Forshaw wrote about the Yorkshire he loved, but he used standard English constantly.

No doubt Charles Forshaw will be remembered as the author of source-books for writers on Yorkshire history, and the members of the Yorkshire Dialect Society will encounter his name in their researches. But his poems, hundreds in number, are forgotten, even though many of his lyrics were set to music during the late Victorian period. The purposes that his writings and many anthologies will serve are of course the provision of introductions to the Victorian mind, and to the books of that small number of Yorkshire writers whose work deserves to survive the erosion of time.

RUGBY LEAGUE FIELD

John Waddington-Feather

Poetry Narrator:—

The rugby field in summer grew buttercups like suns,
Huge childhood flowers that plaited out the sins
Of mills and factories, grew the valley green
From little reaches of the meadows grown
Into farms beyond the boundaries of the town —
A textile town too quickly spawned and torn
A century ago from hill and lovely dale.
The rugby and the cricket fields now deal
The farmland out along the river's course,
And buffet mills and chimneys and the care
Of week-day toil back into the belly of the town,
Thronged with grans and mams and prams that turn
Into the shops and cafs on Saturday respite, while dad
And lad bawl   lung-hard down at T'field.
The ball's away, the game's begun and fold
On fold of faces hurl their beer-soaked breath
And gritty comments from the stands
And terraces, gristled teeth-lopped chins
In unison drop on mufflers, an avalanche
Of disapproval thunders up the field, "We'll lynch
Thee, ref, we will!" — "Clog the sod!"
"Eh, clog that bloody hooker! He's set
On fouling right from t'start!"
"Move! Get moving, lad! Th'art like a fart
Corked in a bottle! Stop that fancy dance
And run! By God — he's scored!" The din's
A frenzied burst of sudden sound, and startled
Pigeons wheel in flocks above the stippled
Hen-pens, where in anguish Homing Sid
Waits patiently to clock his pigeons in. "Sod
Them! Sod them!" loud he wails
As precious seconds drain away in wheels
Of fear high in the sky, but still they cheer,

43

Subsiding only while the kicker stoops to choose
His line of flight and nimbly scoop the hole
That cups the ball. Back he comes on heel,
One, two, three: on tip-toe poises,
Sights the posts and then the ball; pauses
One, two, three again and — thwack!
The ball soars like a bird into the thick
Dense crowd between the posts. "A goal!"
They roar, and eye and ear are gored
Again, assaulted by a battery of sound
And fluttering hands as flickering faces send
Pale nodding semaphores in argument
Or genial agreement through the crowd.

COLLYWOBBLES,
CUCUMBER AND BUMBLE BEES

Kenneth Forster

THE postmark reads "Guide, Blackburn, Lancs." It carries the date June 9th. 1965. It's one of a hundred-and-fifty thousand different postmarks I've collected in over forty years as a collector. And, to me, it recalls the day I walked into this Lancashire post office and chatted for a while to its friendly, country-complexioned sub-postmaster, Bill Bradley.

Guide is a small place. The gazetteer dismisses it in a single contemptuous line: "Village, two miles SE Blackburn, Lancs., with post office."

Busy works of reference have little space to spare for tucked-away places like Guide. They have other things to do. They must outpour fascinating facts about cities and seaports and teeming towns.

But it's the places such as Guide in this world that breathe life and colour into the massive collection of postmarks I have so painstakingly gathered from so many picturesque parts of Britain, and from countries overseas.

In the context of this article Guide is important as an example of the pleasure one can derive from collecting postmarks. Such a hobby can never be dull if one is prepared to picture the people and places behind the commonplace imprint of a postmark on a letter. And postmarks have a habit, too, of perpetuating forgotten facts and putting on record matters of local interest.

When I began to collect postal date-stamps as a school-boy in 1932, my aim was to try and obtain one imprint from every post office in the world. For years I ploughed on, happily unaware that this was a hopeless quest. By the time I discovered that the Universal Postal Union's formidable two-volume register records something like half a million different post offices – excluding places that have been renamed – I was too deeply committed.

I'm glad, now, that I didn't withdraw from my original daft, wild ambition. By simplifying my collecting range to cover the world's far corners I have gathered into my net much fascinating material that might otherwise have had to be discarded. In my files, carefully catalogued on six-inch by three-and-a-half-inch record cards, are postmarks from places with such believe-it-or-not names as Truth or Consequences, Old Wives,

Collywobbles, Cucumber, Bumble Bee, Banana, and Hell's Half Acre.

From within Lancashire's wide-reaching borders I have harvested a mass of fascinating material with links that go back sometimes far into the echoing years of history. Postmarks had their beginnings in England in 1661. It follows that a good collection may enable one to step back in time and read again the hopes and ambitions, hurts and confusions of bygone letter-writers as they set to parchment the events of their day.

It is in acquiring material of this type — for until envelopes became popular, postmarks were inscribed upon the letters themselves — that one enters a forgotten world where, for example, on May 14th., 1776, Mrs. Hannah Dunbabin, a Liverpool widow, addresses herself to The Commander, Queen's Light Dragoons, at Marlborough, Wiltshire. . . .

"Sir,

I make bold to address you with these few lines to beg the favour of you to grant my son, Samuel Dunbabin, a Trooper, furlow to come over to Liverpool as his Father is dead and there is business to be settled that cannot be done without him. . . ."

Who, we wonder, was Mrs. Hannah Dunbabin? Did her letter reach its destination after travelling by mail-coach along England's rutted roads? Was 'furlow' granted to her trooper son? Or had the Queen's Light Dragoons already left Wiltshire to join the forces ranged against Napoleon?

This is one aspect only, however, of a fascinating, many-sided hobby. One may be tempted, for example, to try to trace the link between the twenty-six post offices throughout the world that bear the name Manchester, or the more modest half-dozen or so that duplicate the name Southport in America, Australia and Canada. In research of this kind I have always had splendid co-operation from fellow-collectors, librarians and post office officials — on both sides of the Iron Curtain — in every corner of the world.

Or one may go map-journeying within the county itself for the sight and sound of some of Lancashire's own intriguing postal place-names. Who christened Stacksteads and Watersheddings? How did Barley come to be so named? What happened at Sudden? Who diagnosed Mumps at Oldham? The postmarks of such places are an open invitation to the inquiring mind, a challenge to one's dormant sense of surprise.

I'M YORKSHIRE TOO

Anonymous

By t'side of a brig, that stands over a brook,
I was sent betimes to school;
I went wi' the stream, as I studied my book,
An' was thought to be no small fool.
I never yet bought a pig in a poke,
For, to give awd Nick his due,
Tho' oft I've dealt wi' Yorkshire folk,
Yet I was Yorkshire too.

I was pretty well lik'd by each village maid,
At races, wake or fair,
For my father had addled a vast in trade,
And I were his son and heir.
And seeing that I didn't want for brass,
Poor girls came first to woo,
But tho' I delight in a Yorkshire lass,
Yet I was Yorkshire too!

To Lunnon by father I was sent,
Genteeler manners to see;
But fashion's so dear, I came back as I went,
And so they made nothing o' me.
My kind relations would soon have found out
What was best with my money to do:
Says I, "My dear cousins, I thank ye for nowt,
But I'm not to be cozen'd by you!
For I'm Yorkshire too."

VIEW FROM SCARTH NICK

Alec Donaldson

THOSE who come on Wensleydale for the first time by way of Scarth Nick are blessed folk. They have the privilege of taking beauty by surprise.

"The landscape bares its bosom to the enraptured eye, we take our fill of it, and seem as if we could form no other image of beauty or grandeur. . . ." Hazlitt might have written this with Scarth Nick in mind.

The little cut in the hillside above Preston-under-Scar is approached from the east by a straight but undulating and confined section of the road from Richmond, at the mouth of Swaledale.

Just before the nick is reached vast, bare limestone quarries spread on either side of the road, but they are over your shoulders and forgotten as the panorama of Wensleydale flicks into view so suddenly as to be almost breathtaking.

This, it is true, is only a part of Wensleydale, but it is a good and, some people think, the best part. To me, this is quintessential Wensleydale, one of the finest views in England. It is quite superb, especially when the air is clean washed and dry.

The dale here is wide and generous. It is like a deep bowl held by hills which are ample and inviting. The floor and lower slopes are green, a fine brilliant green. Higher up, the enclosing tops show deeper moor colours. But green predominates.

There is not much ploughland to break into it, for agriculture here is, traditionally, based on grass in pastures and meadows.

Only the deeper tones of the trees provide variety. Shade trees, shelter trees, isolated trees, hedgerow trees and commercial trees create a casual, higgle-piggledy patterning against the lush, jewel-like green of the fields.

The trees even tend to obscure or divert attention from the drystone walls which have endured for long years. This part of Wensleydale has them, of course (after all, it is a Yorkshire dale) but they are not as intrusive as they are, for instance, in Swaledale to the north.

Even further north lies Stainmore. Just where the Scotch Corner-Carlisle road over its summit begins to drop to the west there is another surprise view. It is of the Eden Valley, and it, too, is large and wide and breathtakingly lovely at times.

The view from Scarth Nick in some way resembles it, but while the one is vast the other is a miniature. The detail in the reach of Wensleydale below Scarth Nick is much more precise, much more sharply focussed. The Eden Valley looks remote and diffused by distance; that from Scarth Nick is immediate and intimate.

Away on the left, and seeming to fill the lower sky, is Penhill, long and flat-topped. It seems devoid of features, save at its broad shoulders, where the weather of aeons has attacked and eroded the hill's upper crust to create simple but dramatic lines.

It is the same at Nab End on the opposite side of the dale and, in between but faraway, Addleborough, flat-topped, too, but more graceful, more elegant than Penhill.

Penhill is dominant. It is big, it is powerful, yet more often than not it is curiously two-dimensional. Only rarely does enough light appear to get into its northern face to give it depth. It also tends to impose its own fleeting moods on this part of the dale. Light again has much to do with this, as many artists know.

Fred Lawson, that distinguished water-colourist, made this bit of Wensleydale his own. When he was not pre-occupied with Bolton Castle, that magnificent Scrope stronghold on the northern slope, he saw Penhill as a special problem, and often applied his fine, sensitive eye and mind, and undoubted skill, to capturing in his pictures the hill's changing faces. They were a constant challenge to him.

There is another curious thing about Penhill. Its bulk can vary from day to day, again depending on light. When the sky is overcast the hill seems to grow and thrust up so that it glowers and threatens and almost overawes. When the light is kinder the great mass sinks back and relaxes and takes on an altogether friendlier mood.

From this dominant feature the ground falls gradually down to the Ure. The river is only briefly seen as silver flecks against the green, but almost its entire course in this reach can be traced by the trees that selvedge it.

Then in a fine sweep the ground soars from the valley to Nab End and the tops that separate Wensleydale from Swaledale.

The lowlying land is pricked with the leaden grey of farmsteads and their detached barns. In such a broad scene they lock small and insignificant, though they are vital elements, aesthetically as well as in the area's rural economy.

Even where the grey flecks concentrate to become villages they look small and, sometimes, withdrawn. But, to those who know them, they are warm and friendly places, and they are home to wise country men and women.

There is West Witton, trailing on the skirts of Penhill; Redmire, pleasant and hospitable, to which the Scarth Nick road falls; Castle Bolton, a little higher up the fellside, where in other days one basked in warm friendships; and beyond lies Carperby, long, straggling and old.

Fred Lawson, George Jackson, Henrietta Lister, George Graham, Stuart Milner and Jacob Kramer knew Castle Bolton and Redmire. Lawson had thrust urban temptations aside and painted in this delectable land for 50 years or so. Some of the others were regular visitors to his home.

George Jackson — water-colourist, too — turned to writing plays in Wensleydale dialect and producing them in the dale for enraptured audiences. He succeeded, through his own plays, and others by Dorothy Una Ratcliffe, Florence Bone and Watson Dyke, in crystallising aspects of dale life, and portraying them honestly for what they were.

It is interesting to wonder, looking down from Scarth Nick on to this fair and essentially rural scene, whether any other bit of country could have boasted such powerful impulses in native arts and drama as radiated from Redmire and Castle Bolton in those years.

Redmire's inn then was splendidly welcoming. It had a little parlour, and inn keepers who produced excellent plain country food, even frumenty in season, to warm against singing in the village in the cold night air after closing time.

At the far centre of this view the eye is carried to the junction of Wensleydale and Bishopdale. The unknowing could well be deceived into believing that Bishopdale is a continuation of the major valley. The line of the two at this point is common.

But constricted Bishopdale is to strike south-west, embracing West Burton, Thoralby and Newbiggin before ascending to the tops overlooking Buckden in Wharfedale, whereas Wensleydale turns away slightly north of west to take in Aysgarth, Bainbridge and Hawes.

These little towns are out of sight, but it is comforting to know that they are just around the corner and prepared to welcome those from the urban world beyond Scarth Nick.

Colour in this scene is inconstant. It changes from day to day, season to season. There can even be subtle variations in the dominant green.

There are times when the dale's trees, walls and buildings look warm and rich against the lushness of the fields. Summer and autumn are the best times to observe them in these guises. But there are periods, perhaps when the wind has an edge, or the snow fills the contours or is stouring, or the air is thin and rain-pricked, when the dale seems sombre, colourless, thin, drawn into itself.

All the same, its beauty is rarely sacrificed. If it is fickle, it is always handsome.

Perhaps it is its unpredictability, its inconstancy, that makes the view from Scarth Nick so absorbing, even exciting. I have admired it alone, and in the company of discerning friends who see such things with artists' eyes. The moods of the scene have interested them as much as they have fascinated me.

Unpredictability, inconstancy, provocation! They are powerful stimulants to affection. Perhaps this is why one so much admires this broad, if limited, reach of Wensleydale as seen from the little cut in the hillside above Preston-upon-Scar.

AUNT NANCY

J. H. Eccles (1824-1883)

Aunt Nancy's one o' t'savin' sort,
At niver lets t'chonce pass;
Yet wouldn't do owt mean or low
For t'sake o' gettin t'brass.

Her home's as clean as need be seen,
Whoiver may go in;
An' as for Nancy, dear-a-me!
Shoo's like a new made-pin.

Shoo's full o' thrift an' full o' sense,
An' full o' love beside;
Shoo rubs an' scrubs thro' morn to neet
An' maks t'owd haase her pride.

Her husband, when his wark is doon,
Sits daan i' t'owd arm chair;
Forgets his troubles as he owt,
An' loises all his care.

Wi' pipe an' book i' t'chimley nook
Time flies on noiseless wing;
Shoo sits an' knits wi' pleasant face,
He's happy as a king.

Wi' tattlin' folks shoo's niver seen
I' alley, loin or street,
But goes her way wi' modest step,
Exact an' clean an' neat.

Her neighbours soomtimes watch her aat,
An' say shoo's praad an' stiff;
But all their gossip comes to nowt,
Aunt Nancy's reet enif.

Wi' basket oft shoo walks abroad
To some poor lonely elf;
To ivery one shoo knaws t'reight way
At's poorer nor herself.

Shoo niver speyks o' what shoo gives,
Kind, gentle-hearted sowl;
I' charity her hands find wark,
Shoo's good alike to all.

He niver tells her what he thinks,
Nor flatters nor reproves;
His life is baand wi' gowlden bands
To t'woman at he loves.

God bless her, shoo's a diamond breet,
Both good i' mind an' heart;
An angel spreeadin' light an' love,
That plays a noble part.

Shoo's worthy of a monarch's choice,
Her worth can ne'er be towld;
Shoo cam to mak folks' hearts feel glad,
Shoo's worth her weight in' gowld.

ROSE FOR DAVID

Gordon Allen North

A small boy with a red face, bright blue eyes, and a lick of blond hair that stood up stiffly from his forehead, wriggled uncomfortably in a new, dark suit as he waited impatiently for his mother.

Although it was mid-day, the curtains of the cottage were drawn, and the boy felt uneasy in the semi-darkness.

He wondered how much longer his mother was going to be upstairs, "getting herself ready", as she called it, for grandfather's funeral. The boy had never been to a funeral before. He had no idea what a funeral was; and the prospect of attending his grandfather's greatly excited him.

He smiled to himself, and took from his pocket the silver watch his grandfather had given him after teaching him how to tell the time. It was 1.30 p.m. How much longer was his mother going to be?

The boy had put the watch in his new, dark suit because he knew that his grandmother would ask to see it. Ever since his grandfather had given him the watch he had taken it with him on his visits to the old people.

"Are you taking care of your new watch, David?" his grandmother would ask him.

"Oh, dear, David lad, that watch'll never be thine as long as thi grandmother lives" his grandfather had once said to him, whereupon his grandmother had retorted: "I want David to appreciate the value of things, that's all. He'll be proud of that watch one day."

The boy enjoyed his visits to his grandparents' cottage. He loved the snug cosiness, with its strange smells of ripening fruit, strong tobacco, carbolic, and rubbing lotions. He liked to climb on to the high settle near the hearth and wallow in its solid comfort while listening to his grandfather talking. And he loved to play in the long garden at the back of the house.

During David's last visit his grandfather had plucked a white rose from a favourite bush and pinned it to the boy's lapel.

"There you are, David. What do you think about that, eh? You're like your old grandfather now," It was the old man's practice to wear a white rose in his buttonhole.

The boy remembered a wonderful day in the garden last year when grandfather, after pinning white roses to both their jackets, had said proudly: "We're a couple of real, soil-bred, Yorkshire lads, thee and me, David."

When grandfather's back was turned, grandmother had added a red rose to the white one in David's lapel.

"You tell that grandfather of yours there's some good, red Lancashire blood in your veins, too, David," she had said, loud enough for the old man to hear.

The old man had burst out laughing, grandmother had joined in, and soon all three of them were walking about the garden, hand in hand, laughing loudly. . . .

When David's mother came downstairs the boy noticed that she was dabbing her eyes with a handkerchief.

"What's the matter, mum?"

"Nothing, David, I'm all right. Are you ready?"

"Yes, mum."

"Come on, then!"

They caught the bus outside the cinema. Once the town was left behind it was not far to grandfather's. "Here we are, mum, we shan't be long now," the boy shouted as a row of poplar trees came into view.

The cottage was behind a low hedge. Inside, all the chairs and the long settle were occupied by the boy's uncles and aunts, most of them dressed in black. David tugged at his mother's coat.

"Where's grandfather? he whispered.

His mother shook her head, held up a finger. "Sh. . . darling. Not now, love."

There was a sudden rush among the whispering black-coats as grandmother walked out of the front parlour. She closed the door behind her, and, crossing the room, went into the scullery. The boy slipped in after her. Grandmother was alone.

"Hello, David."

"Hello, grandma – where's grandfather?"

The old woman grasped the back of a chair to steady herself. For a fleeting moment she swayed as though she were about to fall, but she held on desperately. After a few seconds she recovered her composure.

"I – I shall have to explain that to you later, David."

"Yes, grandma."

She looked down at the bright, eager face, with its questioning blue eyes, its tilted chin. However would she tell the boy?

"I see you are wearing your watch, David."

"Yes, grandma."

"May I see it?"

The boy unhooked the watch from its chain. The old woman's fingers closed lovingly about the slim case.

"Have you ever had the watch open, David?"

"Oh, yes, grandma."

"And you've seen the reading inside?"

He nodded.

"Do you know what it says?"

"No, grandma."

The old woman pressed open the case with trembling fingers. She cleared her throat. Then she peered into the watch and intoned the inscription inside. *"Bockley Horticultural Society. Henry Westerman Baxter. Prize Rose Grower. 1923–1929."*

She remained perfectly still for several seconds, bent over the watch, peering down at the inscription. Then she looked at the boy.

"Do you know what that means, David?"

"No, grandma."

"It means that your grandfather was the finest rose-grower for miles around here. Yes, better than anyone in Bockley. And he was the best for six whole years. Six years, mind you, David. And all the other rose-growers in the village bought him this watch, clubbed together they did, and bought it specially for him because he grew such lovely roses. Isn't that a wonderful thing? Aren't you proud of him?"

"Yes, I am, grandma."

"And you should be proud of this watch, too. Your grandfather thought a lot about this watch, and he gave it to you because he loved you. . . " She hesitated a moment, and then went on: "And because he knew that you would look after it for him. You will look after it, won't you, David?"

She closed the case gently and handed the watch back to the boy.

"Oh, yes, I will – yes, I will, grandma."

He stowed the watch away in his waistcoat pocket. A tear rolled down the woman's cheek. The boy watched it course its way through the grey and pink folds of skin. He could not understand why his grandmother was crying.

"Don't cry, grandma," he said.

The old woman looked at him as though she were seeing him for the first time. "Oh, David," she said. She stroked his plump, rosy cheek. "No, I won't cry, love. Your grandfather wouldn't want me to cry, would he?"

The boy shook his head. "No, grandma," he said.

There was a commotion outside the room. A door banged. The boy heard heavy footsteps moving about. Suddenly, there was a rattle at the scullery door, and his mother bustled in.

"Come, grandma. They're here. It's time to go. Come, David." She looked sharply at the boy. "I hope you haven't been upsetting your grandmother."

The old woman patted the boy's head. "Not he," she said. She smiled at the boy. "We've been having a little talk, haven't we, David?"

He smiled uneasily as he glanced at his mother. Then he took his grandmother's hand. "Yes, grandma," he said.

The door of the front parlour was wide open, and big, red-faced men, dressed in black and wearing high, white collars, were emerging carrying piles of flowers. They were taking them outside. The boy saw that the room was piled with flowers. They were everywhere. On the table, the sideboard, even on the little stool his grandfather used to rest his feet on when sitting on the settle. He looked down at his lapel.

"I want a rose in my buttonhole," he shouted.

A hush fell over the room as aunts and uncles turned to stare at the boy. His mother said: "David, David, the very idea, whatever are you thinking about? You can't wear a rose today!"

The boy looked at his grandmother. The old lady hesitated, but only for a moment. Then she walked across to the sideboard, patting the boy on the head as she passed him.

She stood for a moment, looking down at a huge bowl of white and red roses, her thin brown arms and hands poised over the blooms. The assembled company watched her in silence.

After a while she selected a white rose, broke off a little from the stem, and beckoned the boy. David walked across the stood dutifully before her. With trembling fingers the old woman inserted the rose in the buttonhole of the boy's lapel.

"There now, David, that's just as your grandfather would have liked to see you today. He'd be proud of you, I know."

A noisy outburst of coughing and nose-blowing suddenly filled the room, but the boy was too happy contemplating the rose in his buttonhole to notice it.

AH NIVIR CAN CALL HUR MY WIFE

Ben Preston (1819-1902)

Aw'm a weyver ya knaw, an awf deead,
So aw du all at iver aw can
Ta put away aat o' my heead
The thowts an the aims of a man!
Eight shillin a wick's whot aw arn,
When aw've varry gooid wark an full time,
An aw think it a sorry consarn
Fur a hearty young chap in his prime!

But ar maister says things is as well
As they hae been, ur ivir can be;
An aw happen sud think soa mysel
If he'd nobud swop places wi me;
But he's welcome ta all he can get,
Aw begrudge him o' noan o' his brass,
An aw'm nowt bud a madlin ta fret,
Ur ta dream o' yond bewtiful lass!

Aw nivir can call hur my wife,
My love aw sal niver mak knawn,
Yit the sorra that darkens hur life
Thraws a shadda across o' my awn;
An aw'm suar when hur heart is at eeas,
Thear is sunshine an singin i' mine,
An misfortunes may come as they pleeas,
Bud they nivir can mak ma repine.

That Chartist wur nowt bud a sloap,
Aw wur fooild be his speeches an rhymes,
His promises wattered my hoap,
An aw leng'd fur his sunshiny times:
But aw feel 'at my dearist desire
Is withrin within ma away,
Like an ivy stem trailin i' t'mire
An deein' fur t'want of a stay!

59

When aw laid i' my bed day an neet,
An wur geen up by t'doctur for deead---
God bless hur---shoo'd come wi a leet
An a basin o' grewil an breead;
An aw once thowt aw'd aht wi' it all,
Bud sa kindly shoo chattud an smiled,
Aw wur fain tu turn ovvue to t'wall,
An ta bluther an sob like a child!

An aw said as aw thowt of her een,
Each breeter fur t'tear at wur in't;
It's a sin to be nivir furgeen
To yoke hur ta famine an stint!
So aw'll e'en travel forrud thru life,
Like a man thru a desert unknawn,
Aw mun ne'er hev a hoam an a wife,
Bud my sorras will all be my awn.

Soa aw trudge on aloan as aw owt,
An whativir my troubles may be,
They'll be sweetened, my lass, wi' the thowt
That aw've nivir browt trouble ta thee;
Yit a burd hes its young uns ta guard,
A wild beast, a mate in his den;
An aw cannot but think that it's hard---
Nay, deng it, aw'm roarin' agen!

ON GOING SMOKELESS

R. Shaw-Smith

My atlas has a weather map
That portions out the sun;
Red for the countries where it shines
And white for those with none.

For sixteen hundred hours a year
It beats on Beachy Head,
But Bradford and the Aire must do
With barely twelve instead.

Dorset and Kent look nicely baked
And Exmoor and the Weald,
But the shading turns a paler hue
From York to Huddersfield.

Well, never mind; the map may soon
Give us a redder tone
When Keighley down to Doncaster
Is one big smokeless zone.

We've done our bit; it's coke from now
Or pure electric heat;
We'll have the laugh when it's non-stop sun
From Leeds to Simon Seat.

Brass without muck and sunlit moors,
Blue skies the whole year through;
We'll show them yet in Somerset
What Yorkshire suns can do.

FROM A COUNTRY DOCTOR'S DIARY

Will Pickles of Wensleydale (1885-1969)

MOTHER was a schoolmarm by profession. After governess-ships, where she was a great success, judging by the love which her former pupils had for her, she began with her sister a school on the outskirts of Leeds, which had a short life, as an epidemic of scarlet fever killed it.

My mother's character was one of crystal honesty. She was quite incapable of anything mean or shifty. She had indeed a just appreciation of worldly preference, and fought for her six sons like a tigress. Five of us were members of the medical profession and in a fair way to reasonable success. (But Phil, the eldest, was killed when H.M.S. "Russell" was mined entering Malta. He managed to escape from his cabin in the early morning, but, although he gained laurels by working at the full to save the burnt and wounded, was fatally gassed and only lasted a few hours when he made the shore. He was the kindest soul I ever knew, and desperately fond of children, and could always reduce them to mirth and laughter with his simple kindly jokes. One little girl after his death said: "Won't he make God laugh!"

We were very alike in appearance, and his staff surgeon, when I went to the Memorial Service for the "Russell" at Chatham, told me I gave him quite a turn.)

My mother strove on an insufficient income to feed and clothe us, and was in many ways a remarkable woman. I remember her as an advocate for old age pensions to stave off the inevitable workhouse, long before these were put into operation. She never read a paper. I remember her loving sympathy with the unmarried mother, in an age when condemnation was generally the rule.

She had a great pride in her Christmas Eve dinner party, and it would make any modern housewife's head reel. It read like a page from Pepys . . . I remember when 24 sat down to this feast. Eight of ourselves, ten of our cousins with perhaps two or three wives or fiances, and a few friends, including a very Scots neighbour. There was a roast turkey, a roast goose, a couple of boiled fowls and a roast ham, and always a jugged hare; all beautifully served with roast potatoes, mashed potatoes, potatoes in their jackets, Brussel sprouts and cauliflowers, followed by plum pudding seasonably on fire, and mince pies and trifles, and a lordly Stilton.

* * * * * *

My release from the Royal Navy came at the end of January, 1919, and I resumed my happy partnership at Aysgarth with Dean Dunbar. I knew now what hard work really was, and grim toil it has been all these years; but with early rising, and I think I can say good management, a great deal of pleasure was attained---shooting and fishing, tennis and Badminton, golf and gardening. No two fellows could have been happier in their work. We backed each other up through thick and thin, and delighted in the successful practice we built up and kept, and the very happy relationship with our patients. We both despised the doctor who took a delight in coming, as he phrased it, into the 'enemy's country', to attend to the vain patient who liked to boast that he or she had her doctor from some distance, not being satisfied with the local man. The consequence of this was, as we never went out of our area, that our practice was compact, with almost a ring fence, and later, when I took up epidemiology seriously, I found this a great advantage.

The present generation of doctors does not realise what a toil maternity was in those days. There were no district nurses, and the doctor was sent for at the first sign. If the house was a 'bye-side spot', although the birth might be in no way imminent, it was less trouble to stay the night; in bed if this were possible, or in a not too comfortable chair by the fire. As a rule one was made much of, and one's bodily needs attended to, but I could not really eat until the arrival of the babe. Afterwards, the superb breakfasts piping hot from the fire, generally bacon and eggs, were some compensation for one's vigil. There was very little help from the willing but incompetent handy woman, and I have known them faint when I have put on forceps with only myself as anaesthetist. There was no ante-natal care, and the first intimation was that of the night-bell; but with roomy pelves in a ricketless area, it was surprising how little real trouble there was, and how well the majority fared.

* * * * * *

Snow is our worst bug-bear in these hilly districts. There have been few years in which I have not been out on my feet during the heavy snows. My greatest trial, in 1933, was a walk of

63

fourteen miles when the snow was 3 feet 6 inches on the level. I wore gum boots and my feet were frost-bitten on my return. I retired to bed for dinner but was able to resume my tramps next morning. My right foot has never quite recovered normal sensation.

1947 was the worst winter for a hundred years. On the day of the worst blizzard I rang up one of our patients who was recovering from pneumonia, hoping to escape the visit, but heard he was much worse. He had no penicillin, so I set out to walk the four miles. The journeys and visit took me four hours but my heart muscle, even at 62, must have been in good trim, as I ate my lunch heartily on my return after a welcome whiskey and soda.

I had recently engaged a young assistant with a view to partnership and felt the experiences he had had would be enough to warn him off the practice. Far from it; he met all in a sporting spirit, and is settled, and likely to succeed me.

I have had a long experience of snow. As an assistant at Bedale I had several days almost poetic travel in a borrowed sleigh, with bells. Horseback in my early days was the accepted mode of travel; the car, with Parson's chains, was a welcome relief. In 1947 these were never off for eight weeks, and the engine of my car suffered so badly that it had to be replaced.

I could show you a picture of a journey to a house in the snow. In a moment of self-pity, when struggling up-hill, I said with Christina Rossetti — "Does the road wind up-hill all the way? Yes, to the very end."

When snow was thick on the ground those we met had choice of two remarks — "Stormy weather" or "Bad Travelling." A little difficult to understand.

I have walked hundreds of miles in the snow when motoring was impossible or dangerous, and I hope and believe it has been appreciated.

* * * * * *

"SCOURING STONE JOHNNY" lived in Coverdale. He used to travel long distances selling his stones. He lived in manifest poverty, and many a shilling he got from myself and others. In the first war he partially solved the fuel difficulties by removing skirting boards and most of the staircase in the house he rented. He died soon afterwards, and his sister tramped to Redmire with a bag of sovereigns. The undertaker was a really honest man and would not take half of what was offered, and Johnny had what he planned, a first-rate funeral.

He had a truly remarkable imagination, and used to tell a long tale of the Queen coming to Middleham. I only remember scraps, but Johnny told how he met her at Leyburn Station. She said: "Reach down that 'lile' poke from the rack, Johnny. It's a present for thee. We've been killing pigs at Windsor, and I've brought you a few crappins." He escorted her to the waiting 'shandra', a four-wheeled contrivance resembling a Victoria, and took her to Middleham, where she had tea at the Castle, waited on by Johnny, and after other experiences, was driven back to Leyburn Station to catch the last train.

T'DALE WOR MI CREDDLE BED

Gwen Wade

T'Dale wor mi creddle-bed
Pranked wi bent an' primirose,
T'lavrock piped mi birth-sang
　　High into t'blue;
An whiles Ah wor a lile barn
Ah traipsed amang her Marybuds
To souse mi feet in t'fossin' beck
　' An'·t'owd world wor new.

T'fell's bin mi warkstead;
Bi stoany loan an craggy rig
T' cu'lews ticed me ivver up
　　An' nivver let me bahd:
T' clahd-shadders lapped me rahnd
An' t'lev'rets wor mi next-o'-kin,
Wi t'grahse an' pewits hollerin'
　　To t'collie bi mi sahd.

When t'day knocks on to westerin'
An' t'Backend o' mi life is nigh,
Ah'll doddle on wi t'breckon-sleds
　　Dahn off o' t'fell:
May t'robin pipe me hoam to stop
An' t'ullets skrike mi lyke-sang,
An' t'Dale bi mi creddle-bed
　　Wheer Ah sal slummer well.

breckon-sleds	=	bracken sledges
ullets	=	owls
lyke-sang	=	death chant

SHARE AN' SHARE ALIKE   An Edwardian Reminiscence

Ian Dewhirst

I'THEM days — Ah wor nubbut sixteen at t'time — it warn't oft 'at we gat chanct ter hev hawf a day at t'sea-side, 'cos we wor nubbut weyvin'-lasses. Onyhah, me an' ahr Annie went off on t'train wan day ter Blackpool — just fer t'hawf day. After we'd paid wer fare, an' put a tanner o' wan side for wer tea, we just hed a shillin' a piece ter spend.

Well, just as we'd getten off t'train, we saw a chap sellin' sticks o' rock — gert big sticks they wor — an' he wor shovin' 'em inter bags like owt. Me an' ahr Annie'd getten parted, 'cos ther wor a big crahd rahnd. An' Ah sees ahr Annie put her hand up fer a shillin's-worth o' rock, so Ah thowt: "If *shoo* can hev a shillin's-worth, *Ah* can hev a shillin's-worth an' all." Soa Ah gat some rock — gert big sticks they wor, 'cos o'course a shillin' wor a lot o' money i' them days.

Well, when Ah met her, shoo wor carryin' a gert big bag o' rock, an' so wor Ah. Shoo ses: "What's ta bahn ter do wi' all that? Tak' it back ter t'chap." Shoo wor allus a reight bossy 'un, wor ahr Annie.

Ah ses: "Noa," Ah ses, "Ah weant tak' it back. Tha mun tak' thine back."

Ahr Annie ses : " 'Ow's ta think we can goa dancin' terneet if we're boath luggin' gert big sticks o' rock abaht wi' us? Goa on, tak' thine back, an' tha canst join wi' mine."

Soa Ah ses: "Well, thee tak' it back for ma, then," an' shoo ses: "Alreight." Shoo wor allus a reight pushin' 'un, wor ahr Annie.

Soa shoo goas back ter t'chap as wor sellin' it, an' shoo ses: "Sitha, yon's mi sister, an' Ah didn't knaw 'at shoo'd getten a shillin's-worth o' rock when Ah gat mine, so will ta tak' this shillin's-worth back?" An' he reckoned ter looik ter see 'at noan on it wor etten, an' then he tak' it an' gev her her shillin' back — *my* shillin' it wor, o' course, 'cos it wor my rock 'at shoo'd ta'en back.

Soa Ah ses to ahr Annie: "Let's hev mi shillin' then." An' shoo ses: "Nay, tha's bahn ter join at my rock, soa tha mun gie me a tanner aht o' thi' shillin'. Share an' share alike." Shoo wor allus a reight nippy 'un, wor ahr Annie.

Well, onyhah, we gat on ter t'promenade, an' t' sea wor reight rough, an t waves wor comin' splashin' ower t'railin's: but we thowt we'd hev a sixpenny sail. They hed ter get onter this booat – it wor like a big rowin'-booat – from t' prom, 'cos t'sea wor all ower t'sands. An' this booat come in, an' they wor carryin' fowk off 'at wor sick; but we thowt we'd hev a sail all t'same, 'cos we wor reight silly lasses then.

Well, we gat on this booat, an' ahr Annie wor at one end an' Ah wor at t'other, 'cos ther wor a lot o' fowk on. An' t'booat wor bobbin' abaht, an' we wor all gettin' wet wi' t'splashin', an' ther wor a chap wi' a concertina, an' he wor singin'

> "Three women ter ivery man,
> Say, boys, if you can,
> Why shouldn't ivery man
> Hev – – three – – wives?"

for all he wor worth. An' sooin' t'chap 'at wor sailin' t'booat shahted ter his mate ter put t' tarpaulin' up, an' this big tarpaulin cam' across t'top on us, an' t'watter 'at war in it cam' shutterin' dahn on us. An' Ah lewked back, an' does ta knaw, we wor nobbut abaht ten yards frae t'prom, an' we'd bin sailin' fer ten minutes! Then we hed ter land, 'cos t'sea wor really too rough.

Onyhah, ahr Annie cam' ter me after, an' shoo ses: "Ah wor sat bi a chap, an' he paid mi tanner. An couldn't oppen mi purse, 'cos o' t'waves, an' he ses: "Oh, nivver mind, lass, Ah'll pay fer tha." Shoo wor allus a reight bonny 'un, wor ahr Annie. Soa Ah ses: "Well," Ah ses, "tha can gie me threep'nce then. Share an' share alike, tha knaws!"

A DIFFERENT VIEW OF YORK

Dorothy Cowlin

IT is difficult for a twentieth century sightseer to imagine anything much more satisfying than the city of York. It has everything: mediaeval walls and gateways; churches of every possible period; Tudor Guild halls, like the Merchant Adventurers' and the Merchant Taylors'; a fourteenth century tower on a Norman mound; countless Tudor houses with crazily leaning timber facades in a maze of narrow streets with quaint and comic names like 'whip me whop me' — — the lot. We are well-conditioned nowadays to revel in the beauty and the historical fascination of this sort of thing.

It was not always so. One sightseer, of the seventeenth century, recorded a very different view of York, which I fancy may in fact have been the general view in her time. Celia Fiennes, who in 1697 made what was then, for either sex, a most adventurous journey into the wilds of Yorkshire, must have been a remarkable courageous woman to have travelled on horseback, alone except for a servant, up and down the appalling highways of those days.

The journals she kept of her travels show her to have been intelligent, too. Never published in her life-time, or even intended for publication, quite unliterary, the spelling and punctuation wayward to say the least, they make excellent reading today, for the light they throw on social conditions and social attitudes in her time.

The daughter of a distinguished member of Cromwell's party, she never married, though she had hosts of friends, and was comfortably off, if not exactly wealthy. She had money invested in salt-mines in Cheshire, and had, for a woman, an unusual interest in the processes of mining of every kind. Tin-mines in Cornwall, lead-mines in Derbyshire, coal-mines in Yorkshire and Tyneside, are carefully noted in her journals, together with the methods of manufacturing cloth, paper, soap, glass and so on. Anything of a practical nature attracted her eager attention, and the more 'modern' the better.

Perhaps this was why the city of York failed to impress her. In the late seventeenth century the place was evidently behind the times. It had failed to participate in the outburst of trade, industry, science and architecture associated with the age of Isaac Newton and Sir Christopher Wren. It was still more or less mediaeval, and Celia Fiennes had no time for the Middle Ages. She considered that for a 'metropolis', and as the headquarters of an Archbishop,

'York makes but a meane appearance. The "Pavement" which is esteemed the chiefe part of the town, where the market house and the Town Hall stands, is so mean that Southwarke is much before it. The streetes are narrow and not of any length, save one which you enter from the bridge that is over the Ouise.' (Celia's spelling)

I presume that the street referred to is Ousegate. The bridge itself would not be the present structure of course. She describes it as 'built up with houses' — evidently in the style of the old London Bridge.

As for the river 'Ouise':— 'It looks a fine river when full after much raine, but it is but low in comparison of some rivers — it bears great barges, it looks muddy' (true enough to this day!) 'it is full of good fish; we eate very good codfish and salmon, and that at a pretty cheape rate, tho we were not in the best inn, for the Angel is the best, in Cunny (presumably Coney) Street.'

We have to remember of course how many of York's architectural glories had yet to be added. The Assize Courts, the building now used as the Castle Museum, the Mansion House, the Treasurer's House, and many fine Georgian terraces: all these, and others, add style and grace to the original mediaeval and Tudor city. But even so, it seems odd that Celia Fiennes was so unappreciative of the beauty we now see so clearly.

She did admit that 'York looks better at the approach, because you see the towers of the gates and several pretty churches, (sixteen in number) incompassing the Minster, and all the Windmills round the town of which there are many.'

Looking round cathedrals, it seems, was already part of a traveller's duty. Celia was a dyed-in-the-wool 'descenter', as she spells it. But she never failed to make a thorough examination of the cathedral of any town she visited. She climbed the highest of York's three towers — 'and it was 262 steps and those very steep steps. There is a gallery round the middle of the church, where you may go round and look down into the body of the church, and that was so great a distance that the Men and Ladyes that were walking below look'd like Pigmyes.'

She saw the 'well of sweet spring water in the vestry, called St. Peter's Well the Saint of the Church.' She saw a 'large hunter's Horne tipt with silver and garnish'd over and ingraved finely, all double gilt with a chaine, the same given by a Gentleman that also gave his Estate to add to the revenues of the Church on a dislike to disobedient children.'

She saw 'the fine tissue held over the head of King James the first when he came to England', and a 'chest that was triangular fashion the shape of the Coapes when folded in the middle.'

She saw, presumably somewhere within the Cathedral precincts, 'A Mint for Coyning the old money and plaite into new mill'd money', — and actually stamped a half crown herself.

But what really aroused her admiration was the windows — 'the greatest curiosity for windows I ever saw they are so large and so lofty, three storeys high and painted very curious with History of the Bible.' It seems in general it was the sheer size of the place which impressed her — 'I thinke larger than any Cathedral I have seen,' she exclaims, 'bigger than Winchester Cathedral; all the Isles are broad, the people of fashion use them to walke in, and on that account its much pity they keep it not cleaner!'

What would Celia have thought of the recent state of the Minster, cluttered with scaffolding, the organ in eclipse under a polythene blanket, a great mechanical lift shooting up to the top of the tower, little industrial-looking rails and trucks running in and out of the 'Isles', and the bowels of its foundations gouged out and exposed to the gaze of the curious?

I fancy she would have enjoyed it all immensely. She loved to watch work of any kind going on — much more, I suspect, than to contemplate the finished product. The tremendous lift in particular would have excited her liveliest interest and admiration. Celia Fiennes was one of the fore-runners of modern, technological man.

THE INNKEEPER

Arthur Jarratt

Breekfast? Why lass, Ah's nut ungery,
Ah nivver thowt on for ti eeat.
An Ah's breet as a bullace this mornin,
When Ah owt ti be deead o mi feeat!

Last neet — there'll be nivver nowt like it,
If Ah live tiv a hundhred an ten.
Ah've bin changed owerneet somehoo, Mary,
An Ah's capped hoo it happened, an when.

Thoo'll recall that young couple fro Nazareth:
We'd nowheer ti put em id inn:
Well, Ah fun em a plaace doon i coo-shade —
Bud weather was desperate thin:

Sooa, when Ah'd all visitors sattled,
An thoo hard asleep i thi bed,
An lowsened aud Jess frev her kennel,
An wended mi way doon ti shed.

It was clearer nor dayleet i fowdyard:
Ommost midneet it was — moon at full.
Nut a glimmer frid hooses i village,
An snaw covered grund, soft as wool.

They'd ed nowt ti eeat ti ma knowledge,
So Ah browt em a bite an a sup,
An some oil i case lamp wanted thrimmin,
An happins, to lap bairn up.

Then Ah tended ti coos, an ti Jenny,
An Ah've nivver knawn cattle si calm,
An Ah browt some cleean sthraw doon for manger,
Just ti mak seear at bairn was warm.

Ah deeant think they nooaticed me scarcelins,
As Ah rawmed aboot siding spot through.
They wor taen up ti lewkin at bairn —
An it mother es same name as thoo!

72

Sike a wee, conny thing it was, Mary,
Poor bairn! Ommost lost amang sthraw! —
But Ah couldn't distorrb em mich langer,
So Ah left em an stood oot i snaw.

A still neet it was — sthraange an quiet,
As Ah leeaned up agen dooar jamb. . .
Then Ah fancied Ah heeard soond o music,
As thaw stars wor all singin a psalm.

At fosst — well, Ah thowt Ah was dhreemin!
But they'd heeard it at pinfowd an all,
An Ah seed em come runnin doon hill sahde,
An mekkin' their way sthraight ti stall!

It was Rewben, an Shep, an young Davy,
They'd bin up at top tentin sheeap.
They wor towld ti come doon intid village,
Wheer they'd finnd lartle bairn asleeap.

Noo, sthrangest of all was aud Rewben:
Leeavin' lambs nobbut yistidda born!
But all he would say when Ah axed him —
"The Lord'll tak care of his awn!"

Well, summat was dhrawin' me, Mary,
So Ah went in wi Rewb an his men.
We stood a bit lewkin at bairn. . .
But Ah hardlins knaw what happened then.

We went doon on oor knees theer i staable,
Awhahle mother took bairn ov her knee.
An she crooned a soft lullaby ower it,
Tahme we knelt; Rewben, Shep, Dave, an me.

Noo, God's bairns is all on em lovely,
Why, oor awn was a bonny, wee thing.
An Ah play wiv em, noss em, an love em —
Yit we knelt like we would tiv a king!

Sooa that's why Ah's nut varry ungery:
Ah'd like to walk hills all day lang!
Bud we've visitors' vittles ti see tiv,
Varry seean we'll be booath on us thrang.

But fosst, walk wi me doon ti coo-shade:
Ah feel some day, when we've getten awd,
We'll be glad we leeaked efther that bairn,
An fun it a plaace oot o caud.

VICTORIAN REMAINS AT HARDRAW

Harry Mead

ONE of the most rewarding excursions I have made in the Yorkshire Dales was a visit to Hardraw, Wensleydale, in August, 1972.

I had often seen photographs of Hardraw's famous Force. Many books tell you it has the longest unbroken fall of any waterfall in England — about 96 feet. I had read that you began the walk to the fall through a passage at the Green Dragon Hotel. The same books usually mention that brass-band contests used to be held there.

But what I was unprepared for, because I had never seen it mentioned anywhere, was the extent of the Victorian remains at Hardraw. With our three children, my wife and I soon found ourselves on a tour of exploration — and when we arrived back at the pub a couple of hours later, we felt we had re-discovered a lost part of Yorkshire.

The bandstand where the band contests was held is still solidly there for all to see. Contrary to the general impression, it stands not in the main amphitheatre, which contains the Force, but in a green hollow just before the waterfall is reached. Less noticeable are the tiered stone seats for spectators, on the hillside running up from the path.

When I noticed the first of these tiers, I thought it was simply a stone bench for resting on the way. But a closer look reveals whole terraces of seating — a Scarborough open-air theatre long before its time.

This is only the start to rediscovering Hardraw. A well-known attraction is that you can walk behind the slender waterfall. Having done this, you can complete a horseshoe by returning to the Green Dragon on the opposite side of the river. Some people decide to approach the fall on this side, first crossing a bridge near the bandstand.

But what few visitors appear to notice is that just near the waterfall on this bank, a flight of steps leads upwards. The beginning is obscured by vegetation and the first few steps are a scramble. But soon the steps become more regular, and an iron handrail appears.

Alas, the handrail is not shiny from use. But at the end of a short, steep spiral, one finds one's self at the top of the gorge. A stone bench, lichen-covered, offers a rest for the weary. Immediately beyond is the top of the fall, unexpectedly in a charming glade, shaded with trees.

Later, my wife and I were told that a bridge formerly crossed the stream at this point. We stayed on the same side and began to follow the river upstream. Flat rocks of the Yoredale series form a natural pavement by the river's edge for several yards, and then a paved footway leads through the trees by the river banks. . . . It suddenly became obvious to us that when the Victorians visited Hardraw they not only viewed the waterfall and listened to the band. They also promenaded along the river — and this was the way they came.

With increasing interest, my family and I followed the footway, with delightful river scenery at almost every turn. After passing a miniature waterfall, we came to a stone bridge. It appears that at this point, the Victorian visitors could cross the river and return to the top of the gorge.

We continued on, following the paved way through one of a number of wrought-iron gates encountered on the route. We passed another waterfall, a single thread in the centre of a rocky bed, and then reached the foundations of a second bridge, now linked only by two lashed telegraph poles.

It seemed that this bridge, perhaps a mile from the Green Dragon and half a mile from the top of the Force, was the limit of the Victorian promenade. I crossed by the telegraph poles and helped my wife and family over the bouldery stream.

We then started to follow the paved track leading back to the Force on this bank. In places the broad paving stones were washed away, but near the topmost waterfall stood the remains of another stone bench, carefully positioned to give its occupants a good view of the waterfall and of people walking on the opposite bank.

Time compelled us to leave the paved way at the first bridge, following a cart-track to the main road at Simonstone, near Hardraw. On our journey, one or two other sections of paved way had shown themselves — for instance a track leading away from the waterfall at the top of the spiral staircase. We reserved these for another day.

We were also intrigued by a large iron ring set in the riverbed at the top of the Force. Was this where Blondin secured his wire for his famous tightrope walk across the gorge, which was another feature of Hardraw's heyday? You may remember that, to add spice, he tossed a pancake when in the middle.

One can continue the search for Victorian Hardraw in the Green Dragon. It contains a photograph of a crowd at one of the band contests, which began in the early 1880's. They stopped in 1899 after a cloudburst changed the course of the stream, but they were revived in 1920 and finished as late as 1926.

The Green Dragon also has two posters advertising the contests. They note that the track behind the waterfall was wide enough for a horse and carriage — certainly not so today, when the path is narrow and slippery and requires care.

But as you unearth Hardraw's past, it is impossible not to wonder how popular the whole waterfall promenade would be if it were new today. Looking at waterfalls is regarded as a characteristically Victorian pastime. But we seem to enjoy it equally as much. I have no figures for Hardraw, but over 120,000 people visit High Force, Teesdale, every year.

If you love wildness, you might say it is better for Hardraw to have returned largely to its natural state, with only faint echoes of Victorian jollity. One could easily agree that Hardraw's grandeur was diminished by having it turned into a spectacle in surroundings not unlike a municipal park.

Nevertheless, I felt a considerable sadness in finding the Victorian remains so overgrown and neglected. The paved ways were of natural stone, the benches simple, the whole scheme showing a marked absence of fuss. Could we produce anything as sympathetic today, with our apparent desire to tart everywhere up with coy rockeries and rosebeds?

I confess I longed to see the whole layout spick and span and in use again. But perhaps today's crowd, spreading its noise and its litter, would destroy the peace of Hardraw more surely than any of those vanished processions of Victorians, in their high collars or their bustles.

FYLINGDALES EARLY WARNING STATION

(so called)

Brenda H. English

The Ballistic Missile Early Warning Station
Is not, and never was, in Fylingdales;
Though common use of the denomination,
Mendacious and misleading, still prevails.

The Station stands on Lockton High Moor really,
As any ordance map corroborates;
And Lockton's new prosperity has clearly
Resulted from the Station's paying rates.

The world is under a misapprehension,
And grave may be the outcome if it fails
To be informed, by timely intervention,
That Lockton High Moor *isn't* Fylingdales.

Who knows what cataclysmic emanation
May strike the world, and all that it entails,
Because some early warning radiation
Was mis-directed into Fylingdales?

Therefore I beg you, sir, to raise the matter,
And rouse the countryside to agitate;
And Fylingdales especially should natter
With Lockton Moor, before it is too late.

But as for us, although we're not si clever,
An' mebbe haven't travelled varry far,
An' deean't set up ti knaw a vast, howiver,
At t'varry least, *we do knaw where we are!*

HAWORTH OF THE BRONTËS
An unromanticised view

Ian Dewhirst

E ACH holiday season, phenomenal tens of thousands visit
Haworth, The Brontë village', with the steep main street and
famous Parsonage. You hear them babbling with the most
inappropriate epithets, like 'cute' and 'quaint' and 'swell'. How
'romantic' it must have been, they say, living here in 'the olden
days'. Most, of course, do not know what they are talking about.

Not that Haworth, with its two and half thousand souls at the
time of the Brontës, was ever the dead and isolated spot pictured
in popular imagination. In 1853, besides its staple population of
farmers, woolcombers and stone masons, it boasted six cloggers
and eleven boot and shoe-makers, eight tailors and seven
cabinet-makers. There were two doctors, two booksellers, a
grammar school and two rather grandly-named 'academies';
several worsted mills, a temperance hotel, and a tinner and
brazier who also kept the post office. Four carriers provided a
measure of public transport, and an omnibus went to Bradford
and Halifax on market days, and 'to meet trains at Keighley'.

But assuredly, all was not well at Haworth. And in 1850, in
response to a petition signed by 222 residents (who included the
Rev. Patrick Brontë), Benjamin Herschel Babbage came
north. . . .

He was a Superintending Inspector for the General Board of
Health, and his mission was to enquire into sewerage, drainage,
water supply and sanitary conditions. The report of his findings
destroys, finally, any modern notions of blithe old rustic days at
Haworth.

"The face of the country around Haworth is very hilly and
bleak, and there are but few trees to arrest the wintry winds":
Babbage's first impressions read almost like the start of
'Wuthering Heights'. Thereafter he reverted to hard prose.

The average age of death at Haworth, in the time of the
Brontes, was 25.8 years — " about the same as in Whitechapel,
St. George-in-the-East, and St. Luke, three of the most unhealthy
of the London districts." Of every hundred babies born at
Haworth, forty-one would die before the age of six, many
technically from 'causes unknown', because no doctor had
attended them.

Poorer inhabitants worked as woolcombers in their own homes. Combing necessitated a high temperature, stoves kept burning day and night, windows never opened. In a cellar-dwelling at Gauger's Croft, a family of seven slept in two beds in their woolcombers' shop.

There were 316 houses in Haworth in 1850, and only 69 privies (not a single water-closet). No more than two dozen boasted their own; in one instance, twenty-four households shared the same privy; seven in the main street had none at all. One 'perched upon an eminence, commanding the whole length of the main street', above a cess-pit that sometimes overflowed. An open channel, carrying refuse, ran down this same picturesque main street. There were no sewers, just a few covered drains, and most drainage went along surface gutters. The main street was remarkable, at least, for being paved, but there was no public lighting, though gas-lit shops helped to fill the need.

What Haworth lacked in privies, it made up in other quarters: fifty midden-steads and twenty-three manure-heaps, many of these redolent among the houses. A midden-stead at West Lane (next to a row of back-to-back cottages) was heaped with entrails, slaughter-house refuse, and what was graphically described as 'green-meat' thrown out of a butcher's. Farmers were slow to collect night-soil because it got mixed with ashes which detracted from its value as manure. Dung-heaps stank beneath windows, oozed through walls and over floors.

Drinking-water was a rare and dubious commodity. There were eleven pumps in Haworth (including two that were out of order', but few used them for cooking, 'as they do not fancy that this water is pure'. More fastidious villagers would walk up to half a mile for water from the Head Well, but in summer its supply was scanty and on occasion 'so green and putrid' that cattle refused to drink from it. Notwithstanding which, people would start queuing with their buckets at two o'clock on wash-day Monday mornings. An enterprising Mr. Thomas had built a cistern at Sowden's Spring, and piped water to thirty or forty houses at a charge of 3s. to 5s. a year. Pipes and taps leaked, their course being traced by strategic cans catching the precious waste water. One of the taps was within two yards of the over-flowing cess-pit in the main street.

Rather surprisingly – and despite a contemporary diarist's periodic accounts of 'Drunkness' – the consumption of liquor in

Haworth's seven public-houses and three beer-shops, was below the national average.

The Brontës' Parsonage home looked on to a graveyard unalleviated by trees. This was, to say the least, full – there had been 1,344 burials during the past ten years. Most of the graves were covered with flat stones. 'This practice is a very bad one,' Babbage launched into a horrific paragraph, 'as it prevents that access of atmospheric air to the ground, which is necessary for promoting decomposition: and, besides, the stones take the place of those grasses and shrubs which, if planted there, would tend to absorb the gases evolved during decomposition, and render the process less likely to contaminate the atmosphere.'

It was an atmosphere that may well, in part, have killed the Brontë family. Even now, ignoring the crowds and gift-shops, and standing there alone, the observant sightseer may sense its menace. . . .

IN AN OLD FARM KITCHEN

Pavella D. Sutcliffe

In an old farm kitchen, I remember well
Listening to the heavy fall of Bertha's feet,
The lop of water in the pans, where I could tell
That mealy taties soften'd to fire heat.

The hiss of water spilling on red-hot coal,
And rasp of poker on heavy iron bars,
The light tinkle of eggs placed in a blue bowl,
And cock crow to chase away the morning stars.

Timeless, it seems, has been Bertha's noisy rule,
Singing as the springy dough squelched in her hands;
She, a foundling, was left in thunder roll,
Some say by gypsies who had camped on our lands.

In memory I sit with Bertha by the fire---
Water dripping from lines of newly washed sheets;
Singing with Bertha, who never seemed to tire
Of building up the fire with sweet smelling peats.

I can still hear the tick of a little clock,
As it ticked in time to the 'Grandfather's' chime;
They ticked out the day Bertha's hand failed to knock,
The day when her soul to heaven had to climb.

The sound of the hay cart which took her to church,
Sharp ring of the horses' hooves travelling slow,
The splash of the rain from the tall silver birch
On farm kitchen window with no rosy glow.

A FIVEPENNY PIECE

Gordon Allen North

D ICK managed to get two hours sleep in an arm-chair before his mother came downstairs at breakfast time.

"Oh, dear, Mick, I've told you before about sleeping in a chair when you come home from the night shift. Get off to bed at once. Or do you want some breakfast?"

Mick shook the sleep from his eyes. "Some breakfast, mum, please. And I'm not going to bed today. Charlie Hardisty and me are going to the races at York."

"Haven't you to go in tonight?"

"Yes, but I shall be all right. Charlie and me'll have a nap in t'bus."

Mick and Charlie arrived at the Knavesmire in good time for the first race. The sun shone down on Mick's long, curly, blond locks and Charlie's equally long, straight, dark tails with benign impartiality as the two young, 19-year-old nightworkers mingled with the big race crowd milling round the rails.

"Boy, this is the life!" said Mick, gazing delightedly at the spread of green sward. "Say what tha likes, but this is better na t'top 'oil at Joshia's."

"Aye, and it smells sweeter, an' all," chuckled Charlie. He had £4 in his pocket; Mick had £3 in his; and both lads had every intention of spending the lot.

They began by patronising the Tote – and won a pound each on the first race. "It's a start," Mick said, "Th' odds aren't varry good, though. Ah'm backin' wi' a bookie t'next."

"Just as tha likes, Mick," said Charlie. "It's all t'same ta me. We can loise just as easy awther way."

They proceeded to prove the truth ot Charlie's assertion, and, except for the price of a good meat tea, which Charlie had kept tucked away in a purse in his belt, the two had exactly 50 pence between them at half-past three.

"It's all or nowt t'next race," said Mick. He looked at the card. "Sithee, Charlie, ther's a horse here called White Wool. We mun back that. Ah've white wool i' booath yond spinning mules o' mine at Joshia's. It's an omen – or summat."

83

Charlie chuckled. "Ah'm nooan so sure it's a gooid 'un, then," he said. "Ah yerd owd Neddy Battye saying coming down i' th' hoist this morning 'at they wor takkin' all t'white wools out o' t' mules today. They're swapping 'em wi' sum new worsteds. A rush job, he said."

It was at this precise moment that Mick remembered the fivepenny piece. He grabbed Charlie by the shoulders. "What's that, Charlie?" he demanded. "What did tha say?"

"Ah said they're putting sum worsteds in i' t'place o' them white wools tha'rt gabblin' abaat. But what's up wi' thi?" Charlie stared at Mick's paling, agitated face. "Tha looks as though tha'd seen th'owd lad issen."

"Ah've seen moor na th'owd lad," said Mick. "Ah've seen Jack Haigh pooakin' his long nooase raand yond mules o' mine during t'day — aye, an' owd Neddy having a look at 'em befoor Ah get in toneeght."

"What abaat it?" asked Charlie. "They'n looked a pair o' spinning mules ovver befoor today, Ah sud think."

"Its t'draw clock on one o' t'mules," said Mick. "Tha knows, that little brass recorder on t'top o' t'gearing. Ah wor fiddling wi' it last neeght. Ah've done it now — and reyt. It's domino this time."

Charlie stared at his friend. "Ah don't follow thi," he said.

"Tha will in a minute." Mick groaned painfully. "Ah slipped a fivepenny piece i' t'recorder last neeght. If tha wedges a coin under t'finger indicator, t'clock records two draws o' t'mule insteead o' one. It's like putting in double time. Ah didn't tak' it aat befoor Ah laid away this morning."

"What made thi do a silly thing like that?"

"Ta get mi head down. Ah'd a two-hour nap in' t'neeght. Ah wanted to be breet and lively for today. By gow, if Jack Haigh or owd Neddy finds yond fivepenny piece stuck in' t'clock, Ah'm done for. Finished. Ah's be signin' on at t'Labour t'day after ta-morn."

"And 'appen it'll sarve thi reyt if tha are," Charlie shook his head disparagingly. "Tha wor on t'fiddle, if tha asks me."

"Nay, Ah'm nooan having that. Ah fully intended makkin' it up taneeght. Ah've arranged to work through at snap time and during t'morning break. Ah could level it up eeasy enough befoor we lay away at six."

"What abaat t'next race. . . ?" Charlie began.

84

"'T' next race, mi fooit. Ah've hed all t'racing Ah can stomach today, Ah can tell thee. Ah'm on mi way back wom, lad. Ar'ta coming?"

Mick was already striding off the course. Charlie followed at a trot. . . . .

"They've taen t'white wool out o' yond mules o' thine during t'day," old Neddy, the night spinner, told Mick as he stepped out of the hoist on to the top floor landing stage.

"Oh, aye, what have they put in 'em, then?"

"A couple o' worsteds. A bit o' reyt gooid stuff, Ah think. Ah s'll be up in a minute or two to test it. Tak' t'far mule wol midneeght – an' then t'other 'til morn. Tha'll be on thi own ageean all t'neeght – like last neeght. Oh, and keep thi eye on t'cop shaper on th'Asa Lee. It's getting a bit worn – an' needs adjusting. Ah don't want t'cops looking like yo-yos."

"O.K., Neddy, Ah'll see to it."

Mick hurried into the mulegate. After a quick glance round to make sure he was unobserved, he looked at the clock he had tampered with. There was no fivepenny piece wedged under the indicator finger. He searched the floor. There was no sign of the coin. He poked his fingers in among the rods and levers of the gearing, ran them along hidden ledges, but found nothing but fluff and grease. A thin film of sweat spread across his forehead.

Old Neddy bustled in with his reel and began to take a sample of the spun yarn.

"Oh," he said, looking at Mick. "Jack Haigh fun a fivepenny piece i' t'gearing bottom today when they wor swapping over." He flicked a coin in Mick's direction. "Happen it's thine? Has tha lost one?"

Mick caught the coin deftly and held it in the palm of his hand. He probed the coin with his finger nail. He found the groove made by the indicator point. This was his fivepenny piece, all right.

"It must a' been fast i' summat," said the old foreman. "There's – er – there's a mark right across it."

"Oh, aye?" Mick glanced down at the coin. "Aye, aye, so there is – so there is," he said. He slipped the coin hurriedly into his pocket.

Old Neddy took his sample of weft from the reel, re-tied the broken ends on the cops, and put the reel under his arm.

"Ah haven't seen a coin marked like that sin' Ah wor a young mule minder mesen thotty year back," Old Neddy remarked. He took a long, searching look at Mick over the top of his spectacles. *"And Ah don't want to see another!"* he snapped.

He walked briskly out with his reel and sample of weft, leaving Mick staring after him and pressing the fivepenny piece into the bottom of his pocket as if it was a stolen diamond he was hiding.

THE LITTLE PIECER

Fred Brown

The little piecer;
Little---yes. and young---
Young in years, and life---
Not long left school---
Eager to learn and do;
He came to the spinning-room
Which smelled of wool-grease
And warm machinery---
And saw the spinner
And the mules
All awesome to the boy's eyes.

First---the spinner,
Gaunt and lean---
With long thin legs
Which seemed to bend
Rule-like, just at the knees;
A pair of heavy clogs,
Which clumped and trailed
And made a counter-weight
To that unsteady frame;

A drinker's face,
A bulby nose
And very red
Just like a clown,
And eyes which looked
(With lowering frown)
Past and beyond
As though afraid
He might see again,
Things which scared
And had no name;

Then the mule---that
Busy, humming thing,
Which seemed to live
And know---
And faller-jaws
Which went, Snap!
Like that, Snap!
And drew a length
Of twisting yarn
On spindles
Which danced, and hummed
To a frenzied
Whirling tune;

The boy then learnt his trade,
To piecen up the broken ends,
For warp, and weft,
(Cross-band, and open-band)
To tie his knots,
How did they go?
Left over right---
Right over left;

Then the doffings---
When he saw the spinner
On his long arm
Carry away
A pile of cops,
A pyramid of woolly shapes
Wound and formed,
It seemed at first
Like juggler's magic,
As cabalistic
As abracadabra;

Long dreary days
In a gloomy room--
Small wonder he
Watched with delight
A stream of sunny light.
Pouring down
Through a hole
In the slated roof,
And saw the woolly motes
Weaving and prancing
In prismatic coats,
Like light-limbed dancers
Skilled and versed
In the tricky steps
Of quadrilles
Or lancers;

So engrossed and far away
He heard
A clap of hands--
And saw the spinner
Stand and sway
In drunken sternness,
And point, with
Gnarl-hooked fingers
At a tray of broken ends
Which needed piecening;
A passing cloud
Took away
The beam,
And motes,
Defiant, the little
Piecer, whistled a
Few soft notes.

WINIFRED HOLTBY AND THE WASTE PAPER BASKET

Geoffrey Handley-Taylor

IF THE hallmarks of a writer's true craftsmanship are reflected in frequent book references and constant reprints some thirty or forty years after death, then that much-loved Yorkshire novelist, Winifred Holtby (1898-1935), seems assured of a lasting place in the field of English literature. Yet, it is true to say, but for the part the wastepaper basket played in her short life, and for some years thereafter, it may well be that her reputation would not have been so well secured.

No-one was more surprised than Winifred Holtby when during the Christmas of 1911 she looked into the window of a local stationer's shop and saw displayed there her first publication. A slender volume of poems entitled *My Garden, and other poems* had been published at the expense of her proud mother and produced by the well-known and equally well-respected Hull printing-house of A. Brown and Sons. Until Winifred saw the book displayed in that shop window she had no idea that publication had taken place, much less that she was a budding poet.

How did all this come about without Winifred's prior knowledge? Winifred was, at all times, a modest and unassuming individual. Modesty, however, is a word scarcely applicable to her brisk, worthy and domineering mother, Alice Holtby, who throughout a period of years prior to Winifred's eleventh birthday, had been secretly retrieving Winifred's discarded poems from the wastepaper basket. She deftly sorted the contents of Winifred's wastepaper basket each day and carefully collected what, in her opinion, she though to be the best selection of Winifred's verses. Publication of *My Garden, and other poems* during the Christmas of 1911 was intended as a special surprise for the budding poet. In every sense of the word surprise it was!

Many years passed, in fact her short lifetime passed, before Winifred returned of a more than equal surprise upon her mother. Just as Mrs. Holtby in the years 1909 and 1911 had scoured the wastepaper basket for Winifred's discarded verses (the young poet wrote for her own amusement), so had Winifred in the years from 1930 onwards, as opportunity presented itself, also scoured the wastepaper basket used in her mother's study. It must be remembered that Alice Holtby was a country alderman constantly swamped in a positive quagmire of council minutes, sub-committee agendas and masses of other related paperwork peculiar to her aldermanic status. Following periodical sprees of sorting, Mrs. Holtby would dump many items into the wastepaper basket. Winifred, with a measure of cool dexterity, retrieved items of interest and, securing such papers from ultimate destruction, used much of this 'treasure' from the wastepaper basket when creating her monumental 'landscape', *South Riding*. Those acquainted with this remarkable novel, published after Winifred Holtby's death, will appreciate the irony of the wastepaper basket's importance in aiding, at fateful junctures, the establishment of this novelist's reputation.

Although at this point the wastepaper basket had played a curious role in helping to establish Winifred's name, that same receptacle might also have spelt disaster following Winifred's early death at the age of 37. Long dogged by ill-health, this young novelist was too ill to correct the typescript of *South Riding* before she died on Sunday morning, September the 29th, 1935. When, following her gifted daughter's death, Mrs. Holtby laid her hands upon the completed typescript of *South Riding* her anger knew no bounds. In a fit of unbridled rage she demanded that the manuscript be destroyed at once and that the novel be committed to the wastepaper basket. But for the timely intervention of Vera Brittain, Winifred's literary executor, this novel would never have seen light of day.

Developed one stage further, the wastepaper basket theme in Winifred's life took another dramatic turn almost twenty-five years after her death. In 1958 a decision was taken to publish a selection of letters of Winifred Holtby and Vera Brittain. A few days before the final selection of letters was made, as co-editor of the *Selected Letters of Winifred Holtby and Vera Brittain (1920-1935)*, I received a confidential telephone call informing me that Vera Brittain had been daily destroying (after sorting) many of Winifred's finest letters before committing them to the wastepaper basket. The knowledge of this latest wastepaper basket enactment troubled me deeply for many years and I recollect, at the time, it much affected my hitherto high opinion of Winifred's lifelong friend who had so magnificently commemorated the author of *South Riding* in *Testament of Friendship*.

Thankfully one mellows as the years pass, however, for it is true to say that one has time then in which to have considered most aspects of all things — time in which to have looked upon both sides of the coin. Not in the least one has had time in which to contemplate the vices and virtues of the wastepaper basket, that receptacle known to us all which not only destroys but, paradoxical to say, also saves.

MISS BURTON SURVEYS A BATTLEFIELD

Winifred Holtby (from 'South Riding')

SHE, began to frame in her mind a letter to her friend — one of those intimate descriptive letters which so rarely reach the paper. She would describe the Kingsport streets through which she rode, swaying and jolting.

Five minutes after leaving the station, her bus crossed a bridge and the walls opened for a second on to flashing water and masts and funnels where a canal from the Leame cut right into the city. Then the blank cliffs of warehouses, stores and offices closed in upon her. The docks would be beyond them. She must visit the docks. Ships, journeys, adventures were glorious to Sarah. The walls of this street were powdered from the fine white dust of flour mills and cement works. Tall cranes swung towering to Heaven. It's better than an inland industrial town, thought Sarah, and wished that the bus were roofless so that she might sniff the salty tarry fishy smell of docks instead of the petrol-soaked stuffiness of her glass and metal cage.

A bold-faced girl with a black fringe and blue ear-rings stood, arms on hips, at the mouth of an alley, a pink cotton overall taut across her great body, near her time, yet unafraid, gay, insolent.

Suddenly Sarah loved her, loved Kingsport, loved the sailor or fish porter or whatever man had left upon her the proof of his virility.

After the London life she had dreaded to return to the North lest she should grow slack and stagnant; but there could be no stagnation near these rough outlandish alleys.

The high walls of the warehouses diminished. She came to a street of little shops selling oilskins and dungarees and men's drill overalls, groceries piled with cheap tinned foods, grim crumbling facades announcing *Beds for Men* on placards foul and forbidding as gallows signs. On left and right of the thoroughfare ran mean monotonous streets of two-storied houses, bay-windowed and unvarying — not slums, but dreary respectable horrors, seething with life which was neither dreary nor respectable. Fat women lugged babies smothered in woollies; toddlers still sucking dummies tottered on bowed legs along littered pavements. Pretty little painted sluts minced on high tilted heels off to the pictures or dogs or dirt-track race-course.

93

I must go to the dogs again sometime, Sarah promised herself. She had the gift of being pleased by any form of pleasure. It never surprised her when her Sixth Form girls deserted their homework for dancing, speed tracks or the films. She sympathised with them.

The road curved to the estuary again. A group of huts and railway carriages were hung with strings of red and gold and green electric lights like garlands. The bus halted beside it. Sarah could read a notice "Amicable Jack Brown's Open Air Cafe. Known in every Port in the World. Open all Night."

She was enchanted. Oh, I must come here. I'll bring the staff. It'll do us all good.

She saw herself drinking beer with a domestic science teacher among the sailors at two o'clock in the morning. The proper technique of headmistress-ship was to break all rules of decorum and justify the breach.

"Oh, lovely world," thought Sarah, in love with life and all its varied richness.

The bus stopped in a village for parcels and passengers, then emerged suddenly into the open country.

It was enormous.

So flat was the plain, so clear the August evening, so shallow the outspread canopy of sky, that Sarah, high on the upper deck of her bus, could see for miles the patterned country, the corn ripening to gold, the arsenic green of turnip tops. the tawny dun-colour of the sun-baked grass. From point to point on the horizon her eye could pick out the clustering trees and dark spire or tower marking a village. Away on her right gleamed intermittently the River Leame.

She drew a deep breath.

Now she knew where she was. This was her battlefield. Like a commander inspecting a territory before planning a campaign, she surveyed the bare flat level plain of the South Riding.

CHANCE-CHILD

Ian Dewhirst

Ah wonder who thi daddy wor?
Happen nah we'll nivver knaw,
Sowger? fiddler? pedlar? Who?---
He just copped on, passin' through,
Hed his fling i' t'summer grass
An' left a chance-child wi' a lass.

Moppet, nay, it's nowt to thee,
Apple o' thi granddad's ee,
Tinker? drover?---let him be,
There's one thowt 'at natters me:
Is he wiser sin' he cam'?
Does he think o' thy poor mam?

Shoo wer bonny, shoo wer fay,
An' shoo moastly gat her way:
Shoo wer allus one for t'lads,
Louder comp'ny ner her dad's---
But shoo were mi only un,
An' shoo hedn't long for fun.

T'hahse is quiet, nah shoo's ta'en,
It'll noan be t'same agean,
But oh, Ah'm fain shoo's left ma thee
To keep me aht o' misery!
Tha'll stop t'dark fra lowerin',
An' save ma talkin' to misen!

Let fowks say, if they've a care,
Hah we're sich an awk'ard pair---
Owd white grandad, wi' a bairn
'At's no bigger ner his arm!
Nivver mind, child, we s'll fend,
An' tha'll grow up straight i' t' end.

JOSEPH'S CURRANT TREES ('Wuthering Heights')

Emily Brontë (1818-1848)

O N the morning of that Monday, Earnshaw, being still unable
to follow his ordinary employments, and therefore
remaining about the house, I speedily found it would be
impracticable to retain my charge beside me, as heretofore.

She got downstairs before me, and out into the garden, where
she had seen her cousin performing some easy work; and when I
went to bid them to come to breakfast, I saw she had persuaded
him to clear a large space of ground from currant and gooseberry
bushes, and they were busy planning together an importation of
plants from the Grange.

I was terrified at the devastation which had been accomplished
in a brief half hour; the blackcurrant bushes were the apple of
Joseph's eye, and she had just fixed her choice on a flower-bed in
the midst of them!

"There! That will all be shown to the master," I exclaimed,
"the minute it is discovered. And what excuse have you to offer
for taking such liberties with the garden? We shall have a fine
explosion on the head of it: see if we don't! Mr. Hareton, I
wonder that you should have no more wit, than to go and make
that mess at her bidding!"

"I'd forgotten they were Joseph's," answered Earnshaw, rather
puzzled, "but I'll tell him I did it."

We always ate our meals with Mr. Heathcliff. I held the
mistress's post in making tea and carving: so I was indispensable
at table. Catherine usually sat by me, but today she stole nearer
to Hareton, and I presently saw that she would have no more
discretion in her friendship than she had in her hostility.

"Now mind you don't talk with and notice your cousin too
much," were my whispered instructions as we entered the room;
"it will certainly annoy Mr. Heathcliff, and he'll be mad at you
both."

"I'm not going to," she answered.

The minute after she had sidled to him, and was sticking
primroses in his plate of porridge. He dared not speak to her
there; he dared hardly look; and yet she went on teasing, till he
was twice on the point of being provoked to laugh; and I
frowned, and then she glanced towards the master, whose mind

was occupied on other subjects than his company, as his countenance evinced; and she grew serious for an instant, scrutinizing him with deep gravity. Afterwards she turned, and recommenced her nonsense; at last, Hareton uttered a smothered laugh.

Mr. Heathcliff started; his eye rapidly surveyed our faces. Catherine met it with her accustomed look of nervousness and yet defiance, which he abhorred.

"It is well you are out of my reach," he exclaimed. "What fiend possesses you to stare back at me, continually, with those infernal eyes? Down with them! and don't remind me of your existence again. I though I had cured you of laughing!"

"It was me," muttered Hareton.

"What do you say?" demanded the master.

Hareton looked at his plate and did not repeat the confession. Mr. Heathcliff looked at him a bit, and then silently resumed his breakfast and his interrupted musing.

We had nearly finished, and the two young people prudently shifted wider asunder, so I anticipated no further disturbance during that sitting; when Joseph appeared at the door, revealing by his quivering lip and furious eyes that the outrage committed on his precious shrubs was detected. He must have seen Cathy and her cousin about the spot before he examined it, for while his jaws worked like those of a cow chewing its cud, and rendered his speech difficult to understand, he began---

"Aw mun hev my wage, and Aw mun goa! Aw *hed* aimed to dee, wheare Aw'd served fur sixty year; an Aw thowt Aw'd lug my books up intuh t'garret, un all my bits uh stuff, un they sud hev t'kitchen to theirseln; fur t'sake uh quietness. It wur hard tuh gie up my awn hearthstun, but Aw thowt Aw *could* do that! Bud, nah, shoo's taan my garden frough me, un by th'heart, maister, Aw cannot stand it! Yah may bend tuh th'yoak, and ye will — Aw noan used to't, and an owd man doesn't sooin get used tuh new barthens. Aw'd rayther arn mi bite an' my sup wi' a hammer in th'road!"

"Now, now, idiot!" interrupted Heathcliff, "cut it short! What's your grievance? I'll interfere in no quarrels between you and Nelly — she may thrust you into the coal-hole for anything I care."

"It's noan Nelly!" answered Joseph. "Aw sudn't shift for Nelly — nasty ill nowt as shoo is. Thank God! *shoo* cannot stale t'sowl o' nobdy! shoo were niver soa handsome, but what a body mud look at her 'baht winking. It's yon flaysome, graceless quean, ut's witched our lad, wi' her bold een un her forrad ways – till – Nay! it fair brusts my heart! He's forgetten all Aw done for him, un made on him, un goan an riven up a whole row ut t'grandest currant trees i' t'garden!" And here he lamented outright; unmanned by a sense of his bitter injuries, and Earnshaw's ingratitude and dangerous condition.

"Is the fool drunk?" asked Heathcliff. "Hareton, is it you he's finding fault with?"

"I've pulled up two or three bushes," replied the young man, "but I'm going to set 'em again."

"And why have you pulled them up?" said the master.

Catherine wisely put in her tongue.

"We wanted to plant some flowers there," she cried. "I'm the only person to blame, for I wished him to do it."

"And who the devil gave *you* leave to touch a stick about the place?" demanded her father-in-law, much surprised. "And who ordered *you* to obey her?" he added, turning to Hareton.

The latter was speechless; his cousin replied---

"You shouldn't grudge a few yards of earth for me to ornament, when you have taken all my land!"

"Your land, insolent slut? You never had any," said Heathcliff.

"And my money," she continued; returning his angry glare, and meantime biting a piece of crust, the remnant of her breakfast.

"Silence!" he exclaimed. "Get done, and begone!"

"And Hareton's land, and his money," persued the reckless thing. "Hareton and I are friends now; and I shall tell him all about you!"

The master seemed confounded a moment: he grew pale, and rose up, eyeing her all the while with an expression of mortal hate.

"If you strike me, Hareton will strike you," she said; "so you may as well sit down."

"If Hareton does not turn you out of the room, I'll strike him to hell," thundered Heathcliff. "Damnable witch; dare you pretend to rouse him against me? Off with her! Do you hear? Fling her into the kitchen! I'll kill her, Ellen Dean, if you let her come into my sight again!"

Hareton tried, under his breath, to persuade her to go.

"Drag her away!" he cried savagely. "Are you staying to talk?" And he approached to execute his own command.

"He'll not obey you, wicked man, any more," said Catherine; "and he'll soon detest you as much as I do."

"Whist! whist!" muttered the young man reproachfully. "I will not hear you speak so to him — have done."

"But you won't let him strike me?" she cried.

"Come, then!" he whispered earnestly. It was too late: Heathcliff had caught hold of her.

"Now, *you* go!" he cried to Earnshaw. "Accursed witch! this time she has provoked me when I could not bear it; and I'll make her repent it for ever!"

He had his hand in her hair; Hareton attempted to release her locks, entreating him not to hurt her that once. Heathcliff's black eyes flashed; he seemed ready to tear Catherine in pieces, and I was just worked up to risk coming to the rescue, when all of a sudden his fingers relaxed, he shifted his grasp from her head to her arm, and gazed intently into her face. Then he drew his hand over her eyes; stood for a moment to collect himself apparently, and turning anew to Catherine, said with assumed calmness---

"You must learn to avoid putting me in a passion, or I shall really murder you some time! Go with Mrs. Dean, and keep with her; and confine your insolence to her ears. As to Hareton Earnshaw, if I see him listen to you, I'll send him seeking his bread where he can get it! Your love will make him an outcast and a beggar. Nelly, take her; and leave me, all of you! Leave me!"

I led my young lady out, she was too glad of her escape to resist; the others followed, and Mr. Heathcliff had the room to himself till dinner.

RAILWAY TOWN

Walter Nugent Sinkinson

In common with the rest of the country, the West Riding of Yorkshire has suffered at the hands of the Railway cutters. Miles of line have been ripped up; stations, sidings, signal-boxes, engine-sheds and goods depots have disappeared. Towns and villages have lost their services, among them: Cleckheaton, Heckmondwike, Low Moor, Thornhill, Ossett, Brighouse, Elland, Greetland, Horbury, Longwood. The list is too long to enumerate.

Many the men who trod this road,
Who went to work this way;
Who, clock-round, up or down it strode.
But not tonight, today.

Hither came lads who loved a lark,
Who now are grave with years;
Old comrades trudged it, daylight, dark,
Guards, Drivers, Engineers.

As weary went one up the hill,
A fresh man toed it down;
But now the lonely road is still,
And bleak the Railway Town.

THE LUDDITE OATH (from 'INHERITANCE')

Phyllis Bentley

W ILL tha really take the oath, Joe?" asked Mellor in a pleased
tone.
"Aye!" said Joe firmly. He knew now why he had been
so wretched these last few weeks, why he had avoided Mellor and
been unable to whistle any but melancholy tunes. He had been,
at the bottom of his heart, trying to decide whether he ought to
stand in with the croppers or no; he had been trying to persuade
himself that he need not, ought not to, take the Luddite oath; he
had been so racked by indecision that he had hated the very sight
of a cropper because they made a question to which he was not
ready to return an answer. Now that he had made his decision,
answered his question, he felt an immense relief; a weight seemed
to roll off his shoulders, a cloud to clear from his eyes; his
weariness was gone, he felt ready to whistle the night through.
"I'll take it," he repeated.
"Step forward, then," said Thorpe, pushing him towards the
hearth.
Joe stepped forward, and Mellor took hold of his right hand. A
hush fell on the room and Joe, giving a quick look round to see if
any others besides Mellor were to take part in the ceremony, saw
rows of gleaming eyeballs turned towards him. Mellor cleared his
throat, and said:
"What is thy name?"
"N. or M.," observed Thorpe in his shrill twitter.
"Shut up, Tom!" said Mellor crossly. "This is a serious job.
What is thy name?" he repeated, giving Joe's hand a tug to recall
his attention.
"Jonathan Bamforth," replied Joe. His thin frame shivered and
his teeth chattered with the solemnity of the moment, but he
tried to speak in the steady, manly tone which would express
what he felt, and his voice quite rang in the crowded room.
"Art thou willing to become a member of our society and
submit without demur or question to the commands of General
Ludd?" demanded Mellor glibly.
He slurred his words like one who has learned a piece by heart
without altogether understanding it, and this irritated Joe and

made him feel less submissive to the influence of the ceremony, but he replied firmly: "Aye."

"Tha mun say: 'I am,'" objected Thorpe.

Mellor made an angry clicking noise with his tongue. "Am I giving this oath or art thou, Tom Thorpe?" he cried.

"Oh, thou," replied Thorpe. "Thou, George Mellor. Only see thou do it right."

"Thee howd thy gab, then," commanded Mellor. There was a laugh at this, in which Thorpe joined. "Come on, Joe," said Mellor. "We'll start again. What is thy name?"

"Jonathan Bamforth."

"Art thou willing to become a member of our society and submit without demur or question to the commands of General Ludd?"

"I am."

"Then say after me: – I, Jonathan Bamforth, of my own voluntary will, do declare and solemnly swear."

Joe repeated this.

"Never to reveal," continued Mellor.

"Never to reveal," said Joe earnestly, meaning every word he said.

Mellor faltered, released Joe's hand, and fumbling in the breast of his coat drew out a folded paper. "It's long, the oath," he apologised. "I can't rightly think on what comes next." He unfolded the paper and putting both candles together held it beneath their flames, which were almost choked out of existence by lumps of tallow. "I can't see to read by this light," he complained testily, colouring.

Joe, who knew that Mellor could barely read a word of three letters in good print, felt uncomfortable for him.

"Send for another candle," called out Walker.

"Give him the short oath," piped Thorpe.

Mellor's face cleared. "Aye, that'll do," he said. "Say this, Joe: In the name of God Almighty, anyone that enters into this society, and declares anything, shall be put to death by the first brother."

"In the name of God Almighty," repeated Joe sternly and solemnly, thinking of God, of Marthwaite Church and the high clear note of the church clock striking the hour, of the Ire Valley and of how all the men in it were his brothers: "In the name of

God Almighty, anyone that enters into this society, and declares anything, shall be put to death by the first brother."

His voice so throbbed with feeling that for a moment after it ceased there was an impressed silence; then someone exclaimed involuntarily: "Well done!" and there was a chorus of approving shouts.

"Now tha's twissed in," said Mellor, wringing Joe's hand heartily. "And I'm right down glad of it. Lads, we've done a good night's work."

WEST RIDING PUB (from EASY STREET)

John Waddington-Feather

SO, into their foaming mugs again they plunge, head over heels in ale. Fred Finch's win next-door feeds streams of beer into the whirlpool twirl of hangers-on who driftwood to the bright Black Rat awash with booze. Drink goes in by bursting bellyfuls, whole mountainsides of pub-cut sandwiches are munched away, hot sausages, pork pies and mustard-splashed black-puddings. Pickled eggs slide mouthwards by the battery, whelks and cockles keep white molars all a-chomp, and dental plates get bitty with thin crisps, punctuating tap-room cackle with their vulgar crunch. Tippled ale spills wet on noses that lean whippets poke so soulfully beneath the seats. They watch intently legs of all shapes nudge and shuffle on the floor. Listen and you'll hear them whine or bark impatiently from time to time to see their masters' boots scrape dry the foot-rest by the bar. Like all sad dogs they prick their ears when Tom the landlord shouts out "Time!" sweating as he flicks the towels over upright pumps, stiff and straight at last. "Time!" the tills chink heavy back. "Time!" the sombre clock on the wall ticks out through layers of steamy grime.

TOM-TOM

Ann Berry

WE were looking forward to getting the kitten. It was to be a pretty little tortoise-shell queen, like one I'd had when I was a child. It was all settled, or almost settled, and then Fate, in the shape of old Miss Dent, intervened to upset our plans.

One day there came a knock at the back door and when I answered it I found a queer old woman dressed in shabby black clothes standing there, with an old black bag clutched in her hands.

"Do you want a kitten?" she asked, with a quick bird-like movement of her head, and her sharp blue eyes fixed me with disquieting intensity.

"Well – er – yes, we do, "I admitted, then added quickly, "a tortoiseshell queen."

She looked down at the bag in her hand. "No," she said, sighing, "he's only a little black tom, and nobody wants him." The blue eyes darted a sharp look at me again. "But he's got plenty of spirit," she said, and before I could gather my wits the bag was open and a little warm bundle of fur was pushed into my hands.

"He's got to be drowned," she said, "if I can't find a home for him."

So the dream of an elegant tortoiseshell queen flew out through the window, and a little rumbustious black tom kitten came in through the door. We never regretted it.

Tom-Tom was the wildest kitten imaginable and, when his mad moods were on him, he tore around the room, over the furniture, and up the curtains with reckless abandonment, whilst the children joined in his crazy antics and chased him round, shouting and laughing uproariously. I groaned for my ruined fabrics; yet he walked so proudly with his tail held high, washed himself so neatly, and fell asleep so helplessly that I couldn't help loving him.

He was a constant source of interest and amusement to us all, but especially to the children. They dressed him in dolls' clothes, rocked him in their cradle, and wheeled him in their pram, and he bore it all with remarkable tolerance, and even seemed to enjoy it. He was always their pal, and often their comforter; for there were times in their lives, as in the lives of all children, when their little worlds came tumbling down, and they felt that their hearts would break with the sorrow of it. Those were the times perhaps when Tom-Tom was needed most, and whenever I went to their bed-sides at night to make sure that all was well, and saw a little tear-stained face on the pillow and found the warm vibrant body of Tom-Tom held fast in two small arms, I was grateful.

Alas, children and kittens alike have an unfortunate habit of growing up! The time came when the children were away at school, and no doubt I needed a little comfort then myself. Certain it is that from that time Tom-Tom followed me wherever I went about the house and garden, and even accompanied me so far along the road when I went out. It was about this time also that he started bringing me gifts, and I suppose I picked him up and petted him.

One autumn day when I was in the garden, I heard a sort of strangled miaow and, looking in that direction, saw him carrying a partridge in his mouth, which he duly laid at my feet. I glanced hurriedly round to see if there were any witnesses to this blatant act of poaching, and then whisked the evidence quickly indoors. It was a beautiful bird and I accepted it in the spirit in which it was given, though I *did* wonder as I was plucking it about the pellet marks. Two days later, however, there came another gift, and this time it was a quarter of prime sliced ham, still in its grease-proof-paper wrapping.

"Oh, Tom-Tom, you've been raiding someone's pantry!" I exclaimed, and I imagined the consternation and indignation of some neighbouring housewife when she discovered her loss. Anyway she must have shut her pantry window, for after that the gifts were of the inedible variety again.

Some people say that a cat's love is only cupboard love; but I don't believe it, for Tom-Tom enjoys just being with us. He greets us ecstatically when we return from an outing, almost standing on his head with pleasure as he rubs against our ankles, and, if we bend down for anything, he is quick to jump on to our shoulders, where he either nuzzles us, nibbles our ears, or drapes himself like a fur about our necks.

Nor has this anything to do with the prospect of food, for he knows exactly when it is meal-time, and, if his food is not forthcoming, he sits by the fridge waiting patiently to catch our eye.

The back door and the fridge are near together and sometimes we pretend that we don't understand. "Do you want to go out?" we ask, reaching for the back-door handle. Then he touches the fridge with his paw, and his expressive green eyes look at us reproachfully. He rarely miaows, though he purrs at the slightest encouragement. Only in the morning, when we open the door to let him in, is he voluble, giving greeting in return for greeting with a wonderful variety of intonation in his pleasure at being with us again.

Dear old Tom-Tom, with the tattered ears and battle-scarred nose, he behaves with gentlemanly dignity these days — very differently indeed from the tempestuous days of his youth. Yet he still sleeps in the doll's cradle where he was rocked as a kitten, and when he sits upon my knee and I listen to that rhythmic vibrant purr and feel the warm, soft fur beneath my fingers, I remember that day many years ago, when he first came into our lives and into our hearts.

THE MILKIN' TIME

J.H. Dixon (1803-1876)

Meet me at the fowd at the milk in'-time,
Whan the dusky sky is gowd at the milkin'-time;
 Whan the fog is slant wi' dew,
 An' the clocks go hummin' thro'
The wick-sets an' the branches of the owmerin' yew.

Weel ye knaw the hour of the milkin'-time,
The girt bell sounds frev t'tower at the milkin'-time;
 Bud as gowd sooin turns to gray,
 An' I cannot have delay,
Dunnot linger by the way at the milkin'-time.

Ye'll find a lass at's true at the milkin'-time,
Shoo thinks of nane bud you at the milkin'-time;
 Bud my fadder's gittin 'owd,
 An' he's gien a bit to scowd,
Whan I's ower lang at the fowd at the milkin'-time.

Happen ye're afeard at the milkin'-time;
Mebbe loike ye've heerd at the milkin'-time
 The green fowk shak their feet,
 Whan t'moon on Heeside's breet,
An' it chances so to-neet, at the milkin'-time.

There's yan, an' he knaws weel whan it's milkin'-time;
He'd feace the varra de'il at the milkin'-time.
 He'd nut be yan to wait
 Tho' a barguest war i' t'gate,
If the word I'd nobbut say't at the milkin'-time.

fog	= *aftermath*	*clocks*	= *beetles*
slant	= *wet*	*wick-sets*	= *quick-sets*
owmerin'	= *overshadowing*	*barguest*	= *an apparition,*
gate	= *way or road*		*usually a big*
			black dog

SUPERSTITIONS IN YORKSHIRE

Ruth Pattison

FOR a down-to-earth, practical sort of people, Yorkshire folk seem to have always been amazingly superstitious. Quite a volume could be written on the omens, charms, bizarre cures etc. in which they have believed down through the ages, for the number and variety of these are legion. Some of them, it is true, are not peculiar to our county, but they are with us none the less and are part of our heritage. Many of these superstitions and curious bits of folklore still linger on to the present day in country areas especially among the old folk, and belief in them is by no means wholly dead as yet.

The conviction that misfortunes come in threes is one of the superstitions that remain particularly strong. If· you are unmarried, for instance, and have attended three funerals, you must be careful to attend a wedding before standing at a fourth graveside, or you will die single. If you break one object, you are bound to break a second and a third, and this bit of lore goes on to make the sensible suggestion that after the first mishap it's as well to break two trivial items right away in order to guard against breaking something of value. If one death occurs in a village it won't be long, say some of the old folks, before there are two more. Incidentally, regarding this last belief, in our own village of Barmby Moor in the East Riding of Yorkshire, records of deaths shown in the parish registers between 1813 and 1910 confirm that this actually did happen often enough to give rise to, or lend credence to, the superstition. In his book on the history of the village, the late Rev. W. D. Wood Rees writes: "In a hundred and forty-three instances, when a death has occurred, two others have followed within a month. . . . Taking into consideration that the average number of deaths is seven per annum, we may, at any rate, look upon it as a strange coincidence."

Yet another 'rule of three' belief is that if a dog howls beneath your window for three nights in succession, it portends either evil or death in the near future. The dog, incidentally, is but one of the many animals around which superstitions centre, and it seems to me that our forebears had a somewhat awesome attitude towards the animal kingdom, and looked upon many of its number as being linked up in some strange and mystical way with the power behind the universe. Belief in these animal portents used to be extremely strong. Meeting a hare, for instance, was regarded as being so disastrous that people would turn back on journeys, delay visits, even postpone weddings, should such an encounter take place.

The superstition about black cats I have always found rather odd, since although it was thought very unlucky to meet one, it was reckoned as just the reverse to *own* one, and I can't help wondering what meeting one's own black cat would have portended?

Another curious belief concerns sheep. It is said that if in the Spring the sheep yield a good healthy crop of lambs and do well, the same Spring will be unlucky for women having children. One writer has recorded that in Yorkshire, in 1874, it "was a terrible year for farmers and husbands, for so many sheep and wives died."

Omens of ill usually outnumber the favourable ones where animals are concerned, and it is quite a relief to come across the rather charming bit of folklore connected with the donkey. This merely makes the observation that the marks on the neck and the back of the donkey form the sign of the Cross, and that this is indicative of the entry into Jerusalem.

Insects and birds play their part in the world of superstition, too. A hairy caterpillar, for instance, was said to bring good fortune if you threw it over your right shoulder with your left hand, chanting the while, "Good luck, good luck." Treading on a beetle was supposed to bring on rain, and this belief is still strong in some rural areas to this day.

As regards birds, there used to be a strange belief in parts of Yorkshire that if a farmer killed a robin on Christmas Day (I can't imagine a farmer ever killing one at any time), the milk from his cows would be adversely affected; it was lucky to *see* a robin on Christmas Day, provided it was before noon. It was also deemed fortunate to have money in your pocket on first hearing the cuckoo, and I expect our superstitious forebears would be careful to carry a bit of loose change around during Spring, just in case. . .

To see a single magpie was unlucky; two together, quite the reverse. This is odd, to say the least, since it would seem logical to assume that a double dose of magpie would double the bad luck. To see an owl was unlucky, but should you hear it hoot, and then see it, was to be interpreted as a timely warning of some impending evil. A crow found sitting in any part of the churchyard was said to portend a funeral there within the week.

A great many superstitions are morosely concerned with death. To break a looking-glass was said to foreshadow an early death, and a picture falling, if the glass was broken, spoke of death in the family in the very near future. To my personal knowledge there are people who still believe completely in the latter, and are very distressed if one of their pictures falls down. It is still widely held among the elderly that it is unlucky to give anyone a knife as a present: such an act cuts the friendship, breeds suspicion. I myself once witnessed an old lady refusing such a gift until she was allowed to 'buy' it from the giver. This she did by handing over a pin in exchange, for the payment may, it appears, be of the most trivial kind — a pin, a match, a bit of paper — anything, but *some* payment there must be. This same lady will not say goodbye to me on parting — it would be, in her eyes, most unwise.

And there are those, too, I am told, who will neither commence nor conclude business on a Friday. There are those who will not wear green at weddings. Some will not allow a candle to die out: it must be blown out or snuffed, for to let it die would be equal to passing sentence of death on someone of the household. Another strange superstition concerning candles used to be firmly believed, I am told, by fisherfolk in part of North Yorkshire: at one time, no fisherman's wife would dream of winding wool by candlelight, for to do so would have been tantamount to winding her husband overboard.

But it is not only in the hearts of the elderly that superstition still lurks. A teenage girl of my acquaintance was horrified to see me place a pair of shoes on the kitchen table and grabbed them off with alacrity lest the deed bring me misfortune. Another young lady will not have red and white flowers in the house together; for her the combination of the two colours spells death. And, it seems, there are many Yorkshire people, both young and old, who still set much store by the Lucky Bird, i.e. that it must be a dark-haired man or boy who is first across their threshold on New Year's morning. Why this should be considered especially lucky in this day and age I cannot imagine, but I think there may be a strong possibility that it is a tradition that was born in the days when *fair*-haired invaders brought terror to our villages; the days when a fair man crossing one's threshold might have brought great fear, even death perhaps.

And there we have it. With or without foundation, the old superstitions linger on in many hearts and many places. Will they, in a more enlightened age, fade away and die completely? I wonder. Or will the down-to-earth, practical Yorkshire man still cross his fingers and touch wood as he has always done, just in case. . .?

THE LOST TRAIN

Walter Nugent Sinkinson

This is the way the train went,
Her final farewell creep
From doomed and doleful junction,
Her last late tryst to keep.

Hearsed by a smarting steamer
With slightly averted face,
She sorrowed into distance,
A now deserted place.

Time was when children marvelled
Behind each fast-shut door,
Quicker than road we proved her
By half an hour or more.

She'd carry our milk and butter,
More eggs than hens could lay,
Haddock in ice-cooled boxes,
Warm bread and buns on tray.

Apple and pea and parsnip,
Quick chicks all chirpy in crate;
Even a racehorse travelling
To win the Silver Plate.

This is the way the train went,
This sad abandoned track.
Few saw her leave the County,
And none saw her come back.

ROSEMARY FOR REMEMBRANCE

B. Bunker (A story of the Barnsley Canal)

RAIN fell steadily over the town as Sam drove downhill towards Barnsley; visibility was poor. He knew he must be approaching the old lane which turned to the left, with the lovely old canal bridge just ahead. He slowed down, peering through the slackening shower for the lane, and for the view he was returning to see.

Not that he *needed* to return for that reason, for the picture was his, part of himself, to be recalled wherever he might be. For nearly thirty years the picture had been with him, and on occasion, when overcome by fatigue or loneliness, or sheer despair at the impact of 'progressive' man's seemingly abiding hatred of things of functional beauty, his 'picture' appeared, unbidden. Then — he would never know how — the people and events assumed their correct proportions: belief in the indestructibility of beauty, of peace, and of *real* achievement returned, and he was able to assess the loud-mouthed bombasts of this world at their true value.

A wide road turned off to the left, with heavy lorries thundering along. This wide road must be the little old lane which wound up the hill! Bewildered, he pulled his car to the verge — and suddenly it became imperative that before the sun broke through the clouds his picture be recalled again. He closed his eyes. . .

* * * * * * *

There, surrounding the old Elizabethan cottage, was the garden, running up the lane at the back and down to the canal towpath in front. Flowers spilled over the paths, seemingly trying to enter through door and windows; there were rows of vegetables, thickets of berry-bushes and sturdy apple-trees, and a herb-garden in a corner by the hedge. Near the hedge was a small rustic arbour covered with roses and honeysuckle, and from here was a view along the canal with its quietly passing barges, its contemplative anglers, its beautifully arched road-bridge upstream, and its many busy wharves downstream where swinging cranes loaded or unloaded the boats. Beyond, the town rose steeply with rows of houses surrounding busy factories. The garden and the canal provided a splash of beauty in an otherwise rather work-a-day scene. There was constant traffic on the canal, gliding quietly and safely, and no boatman passed without a friendly glance into the garden, with cheerful greetings exchanged – and often a bunch of flowers, a fresh lettuce or a cluster of berries in a cool rhubarb leaf was smilingly handed over the hedge.

From the cottage an invalid-chair carrying a young man was carefully wheeled down to the arbour, Father being satisfied that his son was comfortably settled before taking up his hoe again. Mother, trimming a shrub in the herb-garden, held up a sprig and called: "Rosemary for remembrance, David." Smiling, David opened the sketchbook on his knee, not noticing a small boy peering over the hedge, watching rather timidly from the towpath.

"Good afternoon, sir. What are you sketching, please?"

"Hello, sonny, I didn't see you. I'm sketching old Bob there, grazing on the canal bank. When he sees that young Jim, who is supposed to be watching him, has fallen asleep, he'll trot along to the hedge to demand lettuce leaves."

And sure enough in a few minutes old Bob came along and whinnied softly over the hedge. He was munching happily away when young Jim came to claim him, and Jim in turn was handed a leaf full of strawberries.

"Would you like to see the sketch, sonny?"

"Oh, yes, sir. My name's Sam, sir."

And so began a lasting friendship. Young Sam soon suggested that David might like to go along the towpath to find more subjects for his sketchbook. Short at first, these trips gradually became more adventurous, and many times young Jim jumped off his father's passing boat to help the invalid chair over a rough spot. Sam and Jim learned, during one of these trips, that David was studying architecture in London when one windy day some scaffolding collapsed, throwing David and the foreman to the pavement. David's spine was injured: he would never walk again. He began to develop his flair for sketching, and his quiet courage inspired in more than one person a love of beauty and integrity. Later, young Sam confided his wish to be able to build canals and bridges.

In due course Sam's wish was realised, and he went away to read for a degree in Civil Engineering. Several years later, his studies completed, he returned to the old cottage by the canal. The wheel-chair was empty. David's father, an old man now, sadly handed him a bulky package with "For Sam" written across it. It contained David's sketches of views from the garden, of the cottage, of the canal with its bridges, locks, boats and boatmen, and one larger sketch of two dear people working in the garden, and a small boy peeping over the hedge. On top of the package was a sprig of rosemary.

* * * * * * *

A pale sun was breaking through; Sam looked round to get his bearings. The lovely garden had disappeared; the old cottage was gone; the canal with its channel long undredged, and with rusting cranes on disused wharves, wound its neglected way under bridges half blocked with dumped rubbish, whilst heavily loaded lorries emitting poisonous fumes thundered over them.

Progress! What fantastic, extravagant, inhuman things are done and labelled (by the supremely ignorant) "progress"! .... Well, he had revisited the scene of his picture — and now he had another picture, a picture of ugliness and senseless waste.

He drew into a petrol station, which surely must be on the site of the old cottage garden, and to the attendant who limped over to serve him he said: "Where is the herb-garden?"

He was unprepared for the man's reply, "The herb-garden, sir? It was over there in the corner by the canal. Do you remember it, sir?"

Memories were soon exchanged, Sam admitting that he was the boy who used to push Mr. David's wheel-chair along the towpath, and who, since those days, had spent almost twenty years in various parts of the world building canals and bridges. And he had returned to find that in this old country — alone among the countries of the world — canals which had been deliberately neglected for years were now being abandoned and filled in! To Sam this was absolutely incredible. He was appalled at the lack of vision and sheer vandalism which had permitted the destruction of the Barnsley Canal, that fine waterway so brilliantly constructed by the great engineer, William Jessop.

It soon became evident that the owner of the petrol station was Jim the barge-lad of earlier days; an ageing man now, who had been badly knocked about in the second World War. He had returned to find his father's canal-carrying business jeopardised by the "closure" of the busy Barnsley Canal, which throughout the war had safely and efficiently carried an enormous tonnage of cargo. In a voice seething with disgust, Jim confided that eventually a "burst bank" had been used as the "reason" for abandoning the canal.

"A 'burst' ", Jim added, "which William Jessop would have had repaired in a couple of days."

And so, with a fine canal deliberately closed, Jim bought the filling-station in 1955. "A one-legged chap like me can manage it, sir, and I had to be near the canal, although it *is* officially abandoned."

"Abandoned? Whatever for? Why, this town owes its prosperity very largely to its canal connections. It is an inland *port*, with direct water connection with the seaports. Has someone gone crazy?"

"Plenty have," Jim volunteered. "Over £200,000 was paid out to firms as "compensation" for the abandonment. The fine aqueduct over the valley there was knocked down as fast as they could, though it was a hard job because it was so well built. It cost the taxpayer, one way or another, hundreds of thousands of pounds to *destroy* this economically and socially valuable waterway."

"But this is sheer lunacy, Jim. Were not Members of Parliament asked to stop this idiocy?"

"They were, sir, and some did their best. But some could not care less. Here's a letter I got in reply from one M.P."

Sam took the letter; such phrases as: " – canal in disuse, potentially dangerous. I would much rather see the canal filled in – ." He could read no more. *If* the M.P. had written: "This canal must be modernised and *fully used*," he would have shown that he was a man of vision and intelligence.

Jim turned to serve a customer, and Sam, choking with indignation, walked over to the site of the old herb-garden, where he absent-mindedly broke a twig from a small shrub pushing its way up through the stone paving. It was rosemary. Suddenly he though of David, of his serenity, his courage, his integrity – and at once the importance of these wreckers of the country's assets became, in comparison, pitifully small. And Sam knew now what he must do. He would stay here in England – no more working abroad. *Our* canals needed saving, improving and modernising.

Sam returned slowly to his car, already thinking, planning. . . . And in his hand was a tiny sprig of rosemary.

Rosemary – for remembrance.

A YORKSHIRE ROAD

R. Shaw-Smith

To find the Roman highway's track
That leads from Castleshaw to Slack
Over the bony Pennine Chain
Beneath the ages' sun and rain
Requires a patience and an eye
Both on the ground and in the sky.
You tramp the moor and cross the peat
And try to line the marching feet
Of legionaries come from Spain
And wishing to be back again;
You look for history's aftermath
Upon an aerial photograph,
And scan the likely path of green
Which is to earthbound eyes unseen,
The stony ribbon, unrenewed,
But now revealed by altitude.
You find it here, directing straight
Towards the fort's sinister gate,
But there beyond the Standedge rim
The causeway and the ditch are dim,
And now surveyors make a stay
Before they think they see the way
That Romans, Celts and Saxons trod
Across the heath and acid sod.
They built it true and built to last,
But in the time-eroded past,
And so the road is hard to draw
That leads from Slack to Castleshaw.

Lancashire writers

A GRUESOME GARLAND

M. Allen

A perfect October night last year on the Sabden road — full moon, brilliant stars and midnight-blue sky enhancing the lure of the red flame soaring upwards in the Nick o' Pendle, showering sparks against the looming bulk of the witches' hill. Gaiety and laughter, children's devil-masks, turnip-lanterns and toy broomsticks mimicked poignantly less innocent revels of long ago, when pagan rites, unspeakable deeds and violent death were witnessed by the impassive shape — indifferent yet broodingly inimical — beyond the firelight's fringe. A compulsion to glance furtively over one's shoulder became uncomfortably apparent, for this was Hallowe'en on Pendle — when anything might happen.

The text-book witch as a toothless old hag, flitting about on a broomstick, hellbent on evil errands, contrasts sharply with the theory that she was just a harmless old herbalist, innocent victim of mass hysteria, confessing to impossible crimes under torture. The truth probably lies somewhere in between. A good case has been made out describing witchcraft as the old religion of western Europe, nature worship in its most primitive form, with fertility of crops, tribes and animals of paramount importance in a hostile world as winter brought death to vegetation and despair to primitive man. Even when he realised Spring's rebirth, he remained at the mercy of the fickle gods, who must be propitiated with ritual blood sacrifice and fire — a symbol of the sun's triumph over the powers of death and darkness. Generations of Lancashire folk fertilized their fields by carrying flaming torches round them and scattering the ashes from festival fires over them, taking care to walk clockwise as they went.

Plants played a vital part in ritual, especially aromatic ones, which were heaped on the flames to drug the senses, inspire prophesy and attract heavenly attention. Ancient writings clearly show that the first men to have practical knowledge of plant properties were thought to have god-like powers, and such power was jealously guarded by priestly sects and religious cults; the terrifying power of magic, which has only recently emerged as a recognised medical science.

The witch was traditional mistress of these secret arts, and flourished despite the perils of her profession, for she pandered to the darker side of human nature. The furtive midnight tap on her door might solicit sudden death for a jealous husband or unwanted wife, a potion for abortion or aphrodisiac, a spell for blighting crops, an image to be made *(best beeswax for his honour the Earl o' Derby and have ye the lock of his hair, my pretty?)*

She could satisfy all demands, for she grew the ingredients for distilling her brews, or knew where to pluck them from gallows' foot, noisome ditch or rifled grave, in just the right planetary hour for success. Many 'white' witches were genuine herbalists of course, skilled in the healing arts, and some of their nostrums became respected medicines, born of the cauldron – the classic example being the foxglove, famous for old Shropshire witchcraft and modern digitalis.

But others were accomplished poisoners, well knowing what they were doing, using plants like Hemlock "digg'd i' the dark", sometimes called Kesh or Cess in Lancashire, and used for many a murder since the time of Socrates. The lovely Christmas Rose of legend, alias Hellebore, had a dual personality, for only a witch could recognise the poisoned one among its "fingers like a mermaid's hand." Herb Christopher rewarded the diligent Lancashire witch who searched for it with a crop of baneful berries dedicated to the patron saint of wizards; or she might favour Yew, of longbow renown, sombre killer of the Shireburn heir to Stonyhurst; or Wolfsbane, perhaps the most virulent of all – slayer of many since Roman times, yet still admired today as handsome Monkshood.

Hawthorn and Elder were exclusive to the witch, both very dangerous to sit under on Walpurgis Night. On the other hand, this was the safest night of all to tamper with Deadly Nightshade, the Devil's own plant, for he was so busy titivating for the witches' Sabbath that he might not notice – though prospective meddlers were well advised to have a black hen handy, to make sure of diverting unwelcome attention.

Moonwort provided heaven-sent opportunity to annoy the neighbours by causing their horses' shoes to fall off, being called Unshoe-the-horse on that account. Kedlock, or Ragwort, was not only useful for cattle murrain, but being well-known as the "fairy horse," provided a convenient alternative for the hard-pressed witch whose broomstick had broken down. Her real steed was the Broom, of course, and countless superstitions have arisen round both plant and products from this — most of them of the "doom and gloom" variety that ensures remembrance. The "sweeping curse" was the most terrible in the witch's repertoire, and families have literally fled hearth and home from dread of it.

Fortunately for the hapless wight, quite a number of plants provided protection in all this morass of mischief and murder. Rowan headed the list, under various names like Witchbane or Quicken, its scarlet berries hateful to the witch, against whom crosses of its wood were nailed to house, barn and dairy door. Rue, "sour herb o'grace", was also highly effective, especially when stolen, while Scarlet Pimpernel, the poor man's weather-glass, not only protected powerfully against evil, but also quelled the foulest temper — which explains why "No eye hath seen, no tongue can tell, the virtues of the Pimpernel".

Many others included St. John's Wort, Vervain, Mugwort, Dill, and all plants with "Lady" or "Mary" prefixes, for they were dedicated to the Virgin. Garlic was said to have sprung up in the Devil's footsteps, but was protective against witches and whooping-cough. Wild garlic, or Ramsons, looking lovely, smelling vile, carpets our woodlands in such numbers that it gave its name to several places, including Ramsbottom.

Thus arose the vast and fascinating network of legend and superstition surrounding plants, from remote antiquity to modern times. The widespread taboo against bringing May blossom indoors, the Twelfth Night banishing (and burning) of the Christmas greenery, the Harvest Festival Corn Dolly — all testify to the fact that plant lore and magic are still very much alive, though it it is strange to think there are children growing up who have never known the living flame on the hearth, never roasted chestnuts on a winter's night, seen pictures in the glowing heart of the fire, watched shifting shadows on the ceiling, tried the teenage divination of love — hazel-nuts and high speed-gas just don't work the same magic!

TETHERED ASTRONAUTS

Dorothy Hardy

The night is huge with snow---
Between deep drifts, the house,
Festooned with weighted wires, squats
Like a foundered ship.
Stick-stiff with frost the rowan does not yield
But points its hoary branches to the sky---
A silent sea glittering with distant stars.
Across the ashen street, bright as new paint,
A lamp's light beam is set,
Leaving the alley shadowed, dark as jet:
And I have but to close my eyes to see
Black-stockinged Lowry children, blade-thin dogs,
Crowding, like moths, a gas-lamp's flickering orbit
Where a boy, his clogged feet threshing,
Soars to the moon on a ship of knotted rope;
Its frayed ends, pennants flying, whip the rimed air
As, straddling the stars, he kicks from the iron post.
Pale under gas-light, bird-men gaze, and see
Far worlds that draw them with their mystery.

LANCASHIRE FISH

Peter Wright

I T IS GOOD to have the chance to write about Lancashire's fishing industry because the public tend to forget fishermen. This is no doubt because builders, mechanics, farmers and so on, are constantly seen at work, whereas fishermen out at sea appear remote. Although we know what through-lounges, gear-boxes and pig-sties are, do we feel so happy, for instance, with *deadmen, ships' husbands* and *sweet Willies?* These are, respectively, quayside bollards, agents "married" to a trawler whilst she is in port (one of their important duties being to persuade drunken members of the crew to sail) and a type of dogfish four to five feet long.

Space being limited, let us confine our attention to fish, since of all fishing matters these seem about the most baffling. I'm not thinking here chiefly of a trip to Lune Deeps when, after other passengers had netted a fine haul, I eventually obtained two pathetic dabs caught for me out of pity by the pleasure-boatman; but of Lancashire fish-names.

Historically speaking, many of these come from Anglo-Saxon *(Herring, fluke, lobster, crab* etc.), since fishing, with hunting and farming, is one of the oldest occupations. There are one or two Dutch names, like *whiting;* and Gaelic, like *garve* and *garvie* for the dab (probably from Gaelic *garbhag);* some Scandinavian, like *skate;* and some probably echoic, like *blob* for jellyfish. A good proportion are previously unrecorded, like Fleetwood's *nowdy* for the grey gurnard; and Flookburgh's *sansker* for the dab, and *chandelier* and *cow-kite* for the white stingless variety of jellyfish. Other names, such as *mort* and *parr* for a young salmon, have been noted previously only from other countries - - - suggesting migration of fishermen along with some of their terms. But etymologically the most surprising fact is the very high proportion of French-named fish *(salmon, bream, sturgeon, mackerel, turbot, ray, cockle* etc.), 42 per cent at Fleetwood. We might expect on the Lancashire coast more Manx and Irish names because of the "Belfast boats", but this isn't so.

Some of the names are very descriptive. Off the coast in autumn arrive the *cabbish-blobs,* large heavy jellyfish which float

125

just below the surface and often get entangled in fishing nets. They disappear about Christmas, killed by the frosts. Their name comes from the French *caboche* for head, plus Middle English *blober,* probably imitating a bubbling sound. *Ray luds* are the four jaw and cheek-bones of a ray patch. Compare the obsolete Scottish words *lud* for buttocks. The underlying meaning is something thick and broad. And sometimes fish are personified, like the *sweet Willy* already mentioned, and the *Jack-cod* for a small, young, well-fed, he-cod, generally very tasty. (She-cod are often fat and most inedible.)

Some fish have strange uses and names. The rough skins of dogfish were formerly used by *prentices* for scrubbing cabin floors. In the old sailing-smacks, *stocker* was part of the cheapest fish caught, which was not sold but shared out equally among the crew. The ray is called by younger Fleetwood fishermen the *roker;* and those caught on Roker Bank, a fishing ground in St. George's Channel, take the curiously repeated name of *Roker Bank roker.* The *'olabut* ("halibut") is also interesting. Its name comes apparently because it was eaten on holy days, and the *–but* ending comes possibly from the blunt shape of its head. A *holybut* spelling in the *Oxford English Dictionary* shows that the Lancashire type of *o*-pronunciation was in use right back in 1616. Lancashire fishermen tend to despise cod and prefer to eat more nourishing fish, especially *'olabut.* A particularly useful variety of it has been the *shirt-bag 'olabut,* a baby halibut which could be smuggled past the police-patrolled Fleetwood dock entrance in a trawlerman's *shirt-bag* "black kit-bag". This was in defiance of regulations, which allow him to take ashore for himself only *enough fish for a fry.*

Lancashire fishermen create many language puzzles, and have long been infamous for floundering in their fish-names. Almost 50 years ago, J.T. Jenkins in his *Fishes of the British Isles* had to admit that "the flounder is called the white fluke by Lancashire fishermen", and that they called a common skate a *bluet.*

Our fishermen don't of course, trouble to learn the scientific Latin names because they are not biologists. Can you imagine an *owd saut* ("old salt") saying: "Dissect that pleuronectes cynoglossus, mate"? No, he says: "Gut that witch," using a far more suitable name which comes apparently from that fish's uncanny appearance.

126

Often, instead of the common popular names, he uses his own terms, and can't even agree with another "Lanky" just what they should be. Thus the dab has various Lancashire names--*garve* and *garvie, brit* and *sansker*. So has the young salmon---*grelse, parr, mort, smolt, forky, fork-tail;* and from Lytham, *trout* which is supported by a quotation from the Ribble in the *Oxford English Dictionary.* The fatherlasher becomes *miller's thumb* (Fleetwood), *'ard eyd* (Lytham) and *bull'ed* (Liverpool). And how many passengers, cruising on the 'Stella Marina' recognised that as the biological name for starfish? They probably don't care, and neither does the fisherman, who on that coast calls that fish a *ster-fish, stare-fish, cross-fish* or *crossums.*

Fish-names from other parts of Britian carry no guarantee of recognition in the County Palatine. Yorkshire's *lazy cod* (e.g. at Staithes, for a lean, ill-conditioned, newly-spawned cod) is in Lancashire a *slink-cod.* At Fleetwood the yellow gurnard, called at Hull a *latchet, is a tub* just as the red gurnard called in other parts a *tub,* is at Fleetwood a *sowdyer.* ("soldier"). Note too the angler-fish, only a fifth of which, the tail, is edible, the rest being thrown away. This fairly useless fish is to Hull trawlermen the *monk,* but in Lancashire *divvil-fish.* What a contrast in names! Moreover, the *bret,* which in some places means the turbot, in Lancashire means the brill. Such very local names for fish might easily confuse a stranger.

As for *shillfish,* by far the commonest around the Wyre estuary is the *mussel,* a name fittingly going back to Latin *musculus* ("little mouse") because it is shaped like one. Mussels are unpopular as bait because their softness allows crabs to pull them off the lines. To catch mussels to eat, the fisherman would row near the sands in his round-bottomed *punt,* seeking a *strike* (a "large capture") of mussels, and would drag them up with a *mussel-rake,* put them into bags, and take them to clearer water, as at Wardleys, where they could fatten.

In cockling, the best (though unfortunately illegal,) method is to place a board on the sands and stamp on it, working it with one's feet. This method of bringing the cockles to the surface by suction is forbidden because it destroys the young cockles too. Instead, the Fylde cockler would use a 12ft. *cockle-rake,* knowing where to *scrat* ("scratch") by the *cockle-eye,* the hole made in the sand by the cockle, which is buried about an inch below the surface. Naturally conditions change. About 1,900 oysters were sold in the Fylde at 7/6d. a hundred, and, what is more, you had to give a good count, allowing four free oysters over the hundred every time. You won't easily find such generosity in these mad inflationary days.

Other interesting shellfish include the hermit crab, which Lancashire folk often call *peeler crab, soft back* or *soft 'un;* the *buckie,* which younger Lancastrians call the *whilk; hen-pens,* with tiny shells split like peas and so small that they are sometimes found in the gutted entrails of plaice-flukes; and the lobster. Fleetwood fishermen think that *red as a crab* would be a more suitable term than *red as a lobster,* though they use the latter, because an adult crab is generally red-shelled, whereas a lobster when caught is black.

Finally the shrimp, which is connected with an Anglo-Saxon word *scrimman* ("to dry up")---when you view shrimps on a fishmonger's slab, you can see why. The Lancashire fisherman's *srimp* for this creature is not just his whim, but a long established pronunciation noted in Joseph Wright's 1904 *English Dialect Dictionary.* His *sprawn* for prawn is more unorthodox, and is unrecorded in the appropriate dictionaries. Still, we must believe him, as words are chiefly met in a living context, from people's mouths, not embalmed in a dictionary.

Well, there we are. Only a few fish have been scrutinised. We could just as easily have considered boats, winds and weather, navigation, tides, nets fishing grounds or harbour approaches, and all would have yielded fascinating information. But I hope enough has been said to show that Lancashire fishing, and indeed, all fishing, merits far more attention than usually falls to its lot.

EMBANKMENT TRACK

E. Josephine Penn

Fifty years ago a quaint little one-compartment steam train ran along the bank of the River Douglas from Tarleton into Hesketh Bank station, where passengers disembarked for the main trains to Southport and Preston. On occasions, however, it continued straight through to Churchtown and back.

A bleary oil lamp marked the cindered patch
So proudly designated "Tarleton Halt".
Behind it rose a meadow's shaggy thatch,
Below it, tangs of marsh and river salt.

And there, a writhing belching dragon cub
Would quaff farm produce, dogs and human freight,
Then ply its penny furrow through sparse scrub,
To meet the railway at the goods-yard gate.

Now halt and track lie like a mastless wreck,
Becalmed and barnacled in jade and gold,
With birds and reptiles basking on its deck,
And musky badgers pillaging the hold.

For where man splashed his signature in smoke,
God's name is gleaming from the daisy yolk.

MI FEYTHER'S WALKIN' STICK

Joan Pomfret

WHEN eawr Joe come whoam fro' th'hospital wi his leg i' plaster an' a pair o' crutches lent him on t'National Health, Ah knew there'd be bother.

"Gret lumberin' moth-etten things!" he sez. "Look at 'em! Ah reckon they hed these i' t'Crimea wi Florence Nightingale."

"Well, yo'll ha' to persevere," Ah towd him. "Come on, let's try 'em eawt at t'front," an' we did, but after we'd struggled as far as t'chip-shop one way an' t'Chapel t'other, even Ah could see it wor no good.

"Oh, to hell wi 'em!" eawr Joe brasts eawt, wi a few more words as Ah dursent put deawn on papper. "Ah've nobbut *one* gammy leg neaw — but if Ah try wi these crutches ony more Ah's hev boath mi showlders eawt an' a brokken nose i' t' bargain. Fred next door sez Ah's frame betther wi two sticks."

"Aye, happen yo would, yo clumsy beggar," Ah sez. "An' if Ah con find 'em, yo con hev mi feyther's - - " an' Ah went up i' t'loft to look fer 'em.

Neaw mi feyther hed two walkin' sticks — his Sunday 'un (a reet posh black 'un wi a silver band reawnd th'handle) an' his ornery everyday one. *That* wor a Ash, varra plain an' sturdy, wi a yellowish handle, an' till Ah went to look fer it for eawr Joe, Ah hedn't sin it fer years. . . Eh, mi poor owd dad, Ah thowt, wod a lot o' t'Lancashire counthryside yo covered wi this owd walkin' stick! Ah con remember misel as a little lass on Darren moors, trottin' alung behind yo o' summer Saturdays wi t'larks singin' an' t'cotton grass shakin' — an' winther Sundays, wi t'frost on t'pools an' a wind thad cowd it welly split yor ear hoil. . . .

Yo used this same stick to point eawt t'landmarks i' t'valley; Trinity Church, eawr heawse, India Mill chimbley; an' sometimes, when it wor clear, yo'd brandish it towerts t'say an' Bolland fells an' Blackpool Tower . . . .We poked at peat-banks wi it, an' tested hummocks o' grass i' t' bogs; once at Rocky Brook, yo pu'ed me ower t'steppin' stones wi it, an' another time we hommered on t'door o' Sniddlehill Farm, not knowin' as t'farmer an' his wife ud flit to Tockus. . .

Yo took t'walkin' stick on yor holidays too, — Ah reckon it's tapped it way alung Fleetwood prom a few times, an' covered mony a mile i' t'Ribble Valley an' t'Yorkshire dales. It prodded cows an' waved at tram-cars, an' hooked deawn nuts an' meawntin-ash berries — t'other stick, t'Sunday stick, wor niver tekken onywheer but church or eawt to tay, but bi the lad, if *this* 'un could speyk it ud hev a grand tale to tell o' t'counthry it's sin, an' t'good times it's hed!

Ah reckon it mun be sixty or seventy year owd, an' neaw Ah've gi'en it a rub up it's as solid as ever it wor — "A gradely bit o' wood!" eawr Joe sez this mornin', smoothin' th'handle mi feyther used to grasp so firmly. "Not like them crutches; *they* look as if they've been punched abeawt bi every poor cripple fro' t'Hunchback o' Notre Dame deawnwards! Nobdi ud ever get agatewi *them.*" he sez, "but wi yor feyther's owd walkin' stick Ah con see misel climbin' Pendle agen next summer, Ah con that!"

MY WYNDER

Samuel Bamford (1788-1872)

Where Gerrard's stream, with pearly gleam,
Runs down in gay meander,
A weaver boy, bereft of joy,
Upon a time did wander.
"Ah! Well-a-day!" the youth did say,
"I wish I did not mind her;
I'm sure had she regarded me,
I ne'er had lost my wynder.

Her ready hand was white as milk,
Her fingers finely moulded,
And when she touched a thread of silk,
Like magic it was folded.
She turn'd her wheel, she sang her song,
And sometimes I have joined her;
Oh, that one strain would wake again
From thee, my lovely wynder!

And when the worsted hank she wound,
Her skill was further proved;
No thread uneven there was found,
Her bobbins never roved.
With sweet content, to work she went,
And never look'd behind her,
With fretful eye, for ills to spy;
But now I've lost my wynder.

And never would she let me wait
When downing on a Friday;
Her wheel went at a merry rate,
Her person always tidy.
But she is gone, and I'm alone;
I know not where to find her;
I've sought the hill, the wood and rill;
No tidings of my wynder.

I've sought her at the dawn of day,
I've sought her at the noonin';
I've sought her when the evening gray
Had brought the hollow moon in.
I've called her on the darkest night,
With wizard spells to bind her;
And when the stars arose in light,
I've wandered forth to find her.

Her hair was like the raven's plume,
And hung in tresses bonny;
Her cheeks so fair did roses bear,
That blush'd as sweet as ony.
With slender waist, and carriage chaste,
Her looks were daily kinder,
I mourn and rave, and cannot weave,
Since I have lost my wynder.

THE TIM BOBBIN INN: Machine Breakers in Council.

Sir James Phillips Kay-Shuttleworth (1804-1877)

A BRIGHT light gleamed from the windows of the ground floor. Crossing the threshold, this light was seen to come chiefly from a large coal fire, blazing in the ample grate of the room which served as kitchen, bar, and place of reception for guests. High-backed wooden settles screened the centre of this room from the door, and occupied two sides of it. In the middle was a plain deal table, and on this glasses of beer, and of spirits and water, with some rough hunches of bread and oatcake. Overhead was a frame, the strings of which were covered with the round, flat, thin flakes of oatcake which had dried there. From hooks in the ceiling hung hams and flitches of bacon. The settles were filled with men mostly smoking from long clay pipes; and spittoons, filled with sawdust, lay beside each on the sanded floor. . . .

All seemed weary and worn. "Oi'n allays been agen this rowing and rioting as brings t'sodgers on us poor wavers," said Silas. "What t'farreps have we to do in feyghting wi t'red coats? Connut we creep into t'mills at neet, and smash o' t' iron wavers as robs eawr childer of bread? A bit of a tenpenny nail stuck in t'reet pleck in a machine, ull break it o' to nowt, when th'ingin gets agate. Yo moit crack 'em o', when th'ingin starts i' t'morn, wi' their own steeam. What's t'use o' lettin' t'sodgers get a chance at us?"

"Nay, lads, let's do nowt underhand. We'dn done a pratty day or two's wark afore t'sodgers geet at us. There's summut righteous i'open wrath, for clemming wives and childer, but we're noan thieves to cloak what we done i' t'dark. . . What says ta, Jonah?"

"Oim o' thy mind, Mark. There's nobbut two uses in what we'n done. If these machines can foind wark for o' on us, there mun be moor on 'em by a deal, and we'n towd t'meausters at we winnot clem. But if they connut foind wark for ten times as mony machines an' steam looms as they now han, then, lads, we'n gien 'em notice to quit. They'n getten t'brass and t'edication, an' we'n nother brass nor larning, but we'n shown 'em as we'n Lancashire pluck. We're not t'lads to dee in t'ditch, 'bout kicking. But I'm noan clear which is reet- - - no steam looms, or ten times as mony iron-wavers."

"Then why smash them as tha' has helped to do?" asked Silas.

"To keep t'pot boiling at whoam till t' meausters han fun out t'reet gate. We mun keep t'hand loom jingling at whoam an we han nowt but oatmale, and praties, and buttermilk, t'pig, and t'garden stuff. After this smash we'st ha' wark 'bout flittin' into t'towns, and by-and-by we'st get mills all o'er t'forests."

RAIN IN THE GUTTER

Josephine Hilton

The street is soaking in the dripping wet,
And the long row of stained stone cottages
Huddles beneath the streaming roof slates,
Drainpipes gurgle and chuckle in the soft summer rain,
To the channels of tumbling, twisting rivers
That ripple and bobble
Where the pavement edges the tar-laced cobbles.
Miniature torrents froth in frustration
Round the wrecks of matchbox freighters,
And rumpled old bus tickets, their journeys completed.
A carton is caught and swirls in the eddies,
Collides with the pavement,
Spinning in dizziness a whirling dance,
Clutches a moment a barrier of match-stems
That struggle to hold it but break in despair -
It is swept with the flotsam washed from the cobbles
On the mad, racing runnel of rain-spate,
To plunge through the bars in a last fearful leap,
Down the black throat
To the belly of the singing street grate.

HANDBELL RINGING AT HIGHER WALTON
nr. PRESTON

Walter Mansley

THE 1960's saw a big revival in Handbell Ringing all over the country. Musical handbells were invented in the 17th. century, and should not be confused with Criers' bells. Here is an account of one team's efforts to make good.

"Do it Yourself" is a phrase which can be overworked, but today many people are making their own pleasures and finding that many old ways are good ways.

The North of England is famous for its brass bands and their annual contests, something which has never faded. But the annual Handbell contests, held at Belle Vue, Manchester, until 1925, died out, and with their passing many sets of bells ceased to be used and have remained stored in cupboards, never seeing the light of day for long periods. A full set of bells can cover six octaves (73 bells) but when it became popular to use duplicate and triplicate bells round about 1890, sets became even bigger, with some Yorkshire teams having as many as 177 bells on the table at once. The table is covered by a large mattress to prevent damage to the bells, and also — very important — to stop the note at its proper length by replacing the bell on the table.

A set of bells which had once been the pride and joy of the village hung in the cupboard of Higher Walton school. They had been used only rarely since the first World War until, in 1961, our Church bell-ringers started to take an interest in them. All the leather caps and handles had perished, and broke off readily when attempts were made to ring them, so something had to be done before they could be put to use. The set consisted of 123 bells, a range of 5 octaves, with duplicates and triplicates. Nobody would ever need so many again, surely, but the cost of restoring even a small set seemed prohibitive without an experienced team to ring them.

The bellfounders were very busy with orders for America, where English handbell ringing has become very popular. As our bells were made by Mears, the Whitechapel Bell Foundry was approached, and they offered to supply a "Do it yourself" type of restoration which would provide new handle, cap and clapper leathers, and pivots for 25 bells, two octaves from middle C. This work was carried out, and about the same time, with typical

Northern helpfulness, some music for the Christmas season was offered by Mr. T. Ogden of the Moorside, Oldham, Handbell Team. No music for handbells had been published for many years, but the music used by our old team had been found in the cupboard along with the bells, and, fortunately for us, was written in the same style. This music required more bells, so after some experience, we went back again to the school cellar for another octave and a few duplicates, and, of course, more leather had then to be obtained and much work done to restore them.

Our team progressed with some help from the Oldham Ringers, and then in October 1966 a rally of handbell ringers was held at Norbury, Hazel Grove. Teams from Lancashire, Yorkshire, Cheshire, the Midlands and London took part, and the whole team from Higher Walton, who went to watch, were thrilled by some wonderful performances and a very friendly atmosphere.

This Rally has now become an annual event, held on the first Saturday in May, and arranged by the Handbell Ringers of Great Britain in a different town each year. Teams come from as far apart as Cornwall, Kent and the Lake District. Higher Walton have performed at all the Rallies since the first, with an ever-increasing number of bells – now well over 80 are being put to use, and music arranged by members of the team is regularly used. Some arrangements for 8 ringers may require over 50 bells, one ringer using as many as 10 bells. Strangely, this can seem easier than ringing only two or three bells with long pauses between notes.

We have given performances at Folk Feasts, Old People's Homes, Women's Institutes, and to mentally and physically handicapped people, as well as in churches and schools. This must be true of many of the teams throughout the country. Well over 100 teams are registered with the H.R.G.B. All ages of people can take part in making music in this way, and derive much personal pleasure and satisfaction from so doing. It is not necessary to be able to read musical notation beforehand, and some teams use numbers, letters, or a combination of both. This can be put on one large sheet instead of each ringer having a special copy, and is very useful for schools as it gets quick results.

The correct way to ring for the old Belle Vue contests was from the table, picking up the bells and striking them upwards towards the chin, checking the motion with the thumb against the cap leather to cause them to ring. This system is still largely a northern one; most southern teams ring four in hand, with the bells held two in each hand, up in the air, and therefore not requiring a table except to rest the bells on when not in use. This way can be very effective indeed with as few as two or three ringers, or with quite a large group, but does not get the orchestral effect which table-method ringing can achieve.

ON TH'HILLS

John Trafford Clegg (1857-1895)

Come onto th'windy moors wi' me,
An' let th'world slur away;
An' yo'll ne'er want or need to dee
Afore yo're owd and grey.

Climb fro' yo'r holes, where wayther lies
Black feaw bi every teawn;
An' sit wi' me to watch it rise
An' rush i' music deawn.

Lev reausty forge an' sweaty mill,
Breek wole an' smooky flue;
Wi' breath fro' heaven yo'r wynt-pipes fill,
An' wash yorsels i' dew.

Like layrocks i' ribbed cages put
To sing their hearts away,
I' slate an' stone yo'r souls are shut,
An' pine for th'leet o' day.

Bowd flutthers ᷐ t'bluebell's banner't spear,
Yeth's painted carpet spread,
There's gowd an' silver lyin' here
Enough for o th' folk bred.

Here's rest an' length o' merry days
For ony 'at'll look;
An' beauty's hud bi th'windin' ways
I' mony a fleaur-pil't nook.

Come onto th'moors, an' lev yo'r wark,
An' let him slave 'at will,
I' th'gutthers wheer Dyeath creeps to marl
Who next he's beaun to kill.

Come up wheer yo'r fore-eldthers coom,
Crawl eaut o' th'valleys deep,
An' lapped i' th'scent o' hawthorn bloom
Live whol o ends i' sleep.

An' seaund, unbrokken sleep yo'll have
Aboon th'world's roarin' strife,
An' get moore quietness i' th'grave
Nor e'er yo' fund i' life.

'AN A QUART O' ALE POSSET I'TH'OON'

Mary Smith

"There's some nice bacon-collops o' th'hob,
An' a quart o' ale-posset i' th'oon:

(Edwin Waugh)

THE glossy magazine article headed 'Your Dream Kitchen' caught my eye, and I looked at its illustrations of yards of stainless steel, tiles and laminated worktops, the only signs of habitation being a jar of coffee beans beside a grinder, a string of plastic onions, two red peppers, and a tea-towel and oven-cloth in a matching holder. I never actually *dream* about kitchens anyway, but this cold lifeless expanse made me start thinking in a kind of 'Kitchens-I-Have—Known' fashion; and one thing they all had in common was warmth.

Apart from the glowing range, which was never allowed to go out, there was a feeling of living warmth; this was the heart of the house, a comfortable, homely place, dreadfully unhygienic by comparison with the glossy pictures of today, but a *place for people*. Handy drawers for string and nails, bits of 'crackin' for whip and top, hooks for lamps (and strings of *real* onions) and plenty of room for Grandma's or Grandad's rocking chair. Here they could sit all day, doing any useful jobs they could manage, and keeping a watchful eye on the running of the household and on the younger generation; someone who might get a little sniffy about 'new-fangled ways' but who always had time to listen, to tell a tale, and to provide a pinny-corner to wipe away tears. The back door was always open, and friends and neighbours came and went; only important visitors knocked at the front door and were shown into the parlour.

One of Grandma's jobs was bunching the herbs from the garden- - - thyme, marjoram, sage, mints and parsley were all dried and hung in the kitchen ready for use, adding their fragrance to the air as well as savour to the food. The walls of the buttery were lined with jams and pickles of all kinds, made in season, with the best samples of each always on show at the front, and used last. A large mug of buttermilk with a wooden ladle always stood in our kitchen, a blessing to thirsty children who knew nothing of bottles of 'Pop'.

Bottling jars for fruit were then unknown to my mother, and she preserved damsons by cooking them in the oven in brown pots, without water, until the fruit 'cracked'. When cold, the pots were covered with brown paper, tied down and stored, and the film which formed on the top as the fruit cooled preserved it for use in pies and puddings throughout the winter, tasting fresh-picked when it was used. This method is still used a good deal by people who do not have a deep-freezer.

Before Christmas we were pressed into service every evening, stoning raisins, chopping suet and nuts, and grating apples and nutmeg for puddings and mincemeat. The mince pies were always made in an oval shape, traditionally a reminder of the Manger. Christmas tea with Grandma was a special event, with the white damask table-cloth, the best cutlery out from its flannel wrappers, the china tea-set from the display cabinet, the sugar tongs polished, and the table groaning under the Christmas fare. There were always twenty-five or thirty assorted sons, daughters, aunts, uncles, nieces, nephews and cousins invited to tea; a large round table was set for the children, who had to stand, as there wasn't room for them to sit even if there had been enough chairs, stools, benches and upturned flour mugs, which there weren't. Tea over, we all squeezed into the parlour, where tales were told and carols sung to the accompaniment of fiddle, melodeon and tin whistle.

After the festivities things were quieter, and on winter evenings "eaur lads" would go out with a bull's-eye lantern and a sparrow net on a long pole. The net was put tight up against the hole, and the light shone on the opening to attract the birds; up to fifty sparrows could be caught in an evening. These were killed, and the heads put into a bag so that the bounty could be claimed from the landowners. The going rate was a half-penny a head, and the same for two young birds or four eggs, because of the tremendous amount of damage done by sparrows to thatch and crops. This payment, along with the pennies for rats' tails, all helped the family income. The birds were then skinned and cleaned, and next night we had sparrow-pie for supper, and very tasty it was, too.

My father was the local rabbit catcher, and as small rabbits were unsaleable Mother roasted them, a dozen or so at a time, and we children had one each. She also used them as stuffing for poultry, and they tasted better than the bird itself. We often had rabbit pie, with carrots and sometimes bacon added, and a lovely golden crust; and jugged hare was much appreciated by those of us who liked the flavour. We always had plenty of little rabbit skins for trimming coats and mittens. Father was a mole-catcher, too, and his catch had to be skinned each evening, with each child who was old enough lending a hand; when the skins were off they had to be stretched square and tacked on to a big board, fur side down. These boards had to be put out in the fresh air each day especially in the frost, but the skins had never to be allowed to get wet. When they were cured they were carefully removed from the boards, packed, and sent off to London furriers.

The boys went "bobbin' for snigs" after a heavy rainfall. They would watch the dyke for a 'fresh', and if they had no eel spear they fastened worms on to a long pole and caught the eels as they came down in the rush of water. That meant snig-pie, a great favourite.

All this messing about around water, and being out in the night air, never seemed to do us any harm, for we were rarely ill. Perhaps the credit should go to the old-fashioned remedies, the idea being then that prevention was better than cure, and that what cured should also prevent! There was linseed and liquorice boiled with sugar candy for colds; melted bacon fat and treacle for coughs; and 'turnip-rum' for sore throats; this was made by sprinkling sugar over sliced turnip, then pouring off the liquid produced. There were many of these remedies- - - powdered chalk in water was drunk to remove warts (and if that didn't work you could always get them charmed away!)- - - a teaspoonful of cuttle fish powder in a glass of water each day was a cure for boils. Nettle stings were used for curing dermatitis, and columbo root brewed in boiling water, cooled, and drunk night and morning, was good for various skin troubles. All cuts, bumps and grazes were soothed with marshmallow salve- - - just before flowering the leaves were snipped and boiled in a minimum of water until tender, then sieved and mixed with pure lard or unsalted butter and sealed in jars. All winter we were accompanied by the rustling of the brown paper covering our goose-greased chests, paper and grease being renewed weekly. This, combined with the onion in a bag worn round the neck to prevent "catching germs", probably gave us a peculiar odour, but our best friends never told us. They probably smelt the same; after all, they all had mothers and grandmas, too!

All this preserving, medicine-making, fur curing etc. was Mother's responsibility when she wasn't cooking, cleaning, making or mending clothes , feeding hens and pigs, milking or making butter. We all had to help according to age and ability, especially we girls, as the boys had outside work to do. I hated washing day with the dolly-tub and posser, and the huge wooden mangle; baking day at least seemed to have something to show for the work. After making bread we made boiled dough dumplings with small pieces of dough, lovely with syrup or jam; "madam flats" were like apple pie baked on a flat sheet, but with cooked apple filling; and "pig in a poke" was a suet roly-poly filled with chopped bacon, and made a delicious winter meal. For breakfast we always had porridge with syrup or treacle, or brewis (pronounced browers) which was pieces of hard oat cake in hot milk; this last was also a supper dish with the milk replaced by meat stew.

There was beer to brew once a fortnight, weaker in summer so that men at the hay-making and threshing could keep having a refreshing drink at their very thirsty work. For a special treat in summer Mother made lemon syrup; lump sugar boiled in water, with lemon essence and tartaric acid added when cool; this kept for weeks in bottles. Mulled ale was prepared for men coming in from work on cold, wet days, and recovery from illness was helped along with a caudle, like mulled ale, but with beaten eggs added.

All these many and varied activities went on in our kitchen; the only things not encouraged to occur there were birth and death, bed being considered the proper place for these, but from early morning the kitchen buzzed with every other sort of happening, and at night we played games (quietly!) while Father read the paper and Mother knitted the endless stream of socks needed for a growing family with the soft light of the oil lamp on the big solid wooden table. The chenille cover, put on after tea, provided ample space for the youngest to make dens or houses underneath. Even at its tidiest, when everyone had gone to bed and only a glimmer from the banked-up fire shone on the pegged rugs and stone flags, our kitchen never looked anything like that one in the magazine. And I'm glad.

SUNDERLAND POINT

Margaret Greenhalgh

If you should wish for peace and rest
With sun and salty breezes blessed,
Come then to quiet Sunderland,
The lonely Point across the sand.

A smuggler's haunt along the shore,
Five cottages, a tiny store;
A place to while the time away
While sea-birds call the livelong day.

A bell-tower with a crazy chime,
A dreaming hamlet lost in time,
Where twice a day as tides may be
You are beleagured by the sea.

A little beach with upturned boats
Where fishermen have left their floats
Like witches' balls of emerald glass
Among the waving marram grass.

SPO

Norman Turner

I HAVE never been able to fathom why certain children's games and customs surface at particular times of the year. Of course, pastimes like sledging and playing conkers are governed by seasonal conditions, but what is it that urges youngsters to get out their marbles, say, or what was it- - - for the custom has declined- - - that prompted them to start surging round the playgrounds with hoops?

Perhaps it was and is no more than a slight lift in the temperature as Spring swings into Summer, and children start to think of outdoor activities that have not been so practicable in chill Winter.

This is almost certainly the reason why you start to see the occasional bottle of Spo when the sun begins to shed some genuine warmth in the months of April and May. Spo, you say, what's that?

You may not know it by that name in every part of the Pennines, but certainly it is still called Spo in many of the villages. And even where it is given no name, there are many folk who remember taking a swig of a dark brown liquid made of nothing more compound than a lump of liquorice shaken up in a medicine bottle filled with water! I knew Spo as a youngster in a small Pennine village, and recall with nostalgia the vigorous shaking that produced the desirable dark brown liquid which memory tells me had all more strength and flavour than many a present-day bottle of pop.

Spo Sunday

The liquorice was the black brittle stuff we bought at the chemist's or herbalist's. A penn'orth lasted for ages, for as soon as one bottle vanished down a clamouring throat we just filled up with water, shook it again like mad, and there was a fresh supply!

Spring was always the time of year for Spo, or whatever other name was given to it, to make its appearance. How it all started, we have no idea, but there are some written records to show that the custom of drinking it is anything but modern.

There actually *was* a Spo Sunday — the first Sunday in May. It was certainly observed in Pennine areas, with groups of young men and women leaving the valley floors and taking to the hills. They would make for the pools which history had named Spo Ponds, and there they would enjoy themselves with the sort of larking about which has ever been the prerogative of the young.

Booth Dean Spa near Halifax was one such centre. Over 200 years ago, it is recorded, this spot was a rendezvous for these gatherings. Later, though, Spo Sunday became a day devoted to Temperance rallies--- an obvious association of ideas, and possibly a natural development of the water rites that must have been practised in our hills for centuries.

Every year as the days lengthened, villagers would celebrate the passing of winter and rebirth of nature. We note the transition these days with the Easter egg and a Christian connotation, but water, too, had its part in these rites. No growth could take place without it, and mountain springs would be natural centres of celebration.

Spo or Spaw?

Our 'Spo' is known as Spaw in some places, and this gives a clue to the origin of the name. It is a corruption of 'Spa', well enough known when associated with place-names like Harrogate, Cheltenham and Buxton. It means a watering place, and is derived from the Belgian place of that name. Perhaps when spring waters were drunk neat it reminded people of Spa waters, and so was given the name. We can only guess when and why liquorice came into use. Was it to add a little "body" to the drink, or was it to disguise the taste of some brackish liquid from a distant peat-bound pond?

Just as Moses sweetened the water of the wilderness by casting a tree into it, so our ancestors may have made their pond water palatable by adding herbs. Since liquorice was produced around Pontefract, here was a ready supply of suitable additive which had the extra quality of imparting colour to the drink.

All is theory--- but a better answer has yet to be found. If readers ponder about this, it is worth noting that in parts of Derbyshire the pagan practice of water worship has developed into the much-publicised well-dressings, and until recent times at Easter the children in the Peak District drank water coloured and flavoured with burnt sugar!

There is a remarkable similarity here to the Spo of the Lancashire/Yorkshire border.

149

Children who still enjoy Spo know little or nothing of all this. To them Spo is simply a drink that can be made cheaply, and is all the more enjoyable because they make it themselves. It needs no psychologist to enumerate reasons. I was strangely pleased when my own children carried on the old custom without any family prompting. It was a natural acceptance of a folk custom.

Spo is not as popular these days as it was when I was a youngster, perhaps because then we had no spare money to lavish on a bottle of pop. I don't think we were any the worse for that.

And at least Spo had one claim that could not be challenged. In its simplest form, it was a "mineral" water long before our modern concoctions!

MY PIECE IS O' BU' WOVEN EAWT

Richard Rome Bealey (1828-1887)

My "piece" is o' bu' woven eawt,
My wark is welly done:
Aw've treddled at it day by day,
Sin' th'toime 'ut aw begun.
Aw've sat i' th'loom-heawse long enough,
An' made th'owd shuttle fly;
An' neaw aw'm fain to stop it off,
An' lay mi weyvin' by.

Aw dunnot know heaw th'piece is done;
Aw'm fear'd it's marred enough;
Bu' th'warps weren't made o' th'best o' yarn,
An' th'weft were nobbut rough.
Aw've been some bother'd neaw an' then
Wi' knots an' breakin' too;
They'n hampered me so mich at toimes
Aw've scarce known what to do.

Bu' th'Mester's just, an' weel He knows
'Ut th'yarn were none so good;
He winna bate me when he sees
Aw've done as weel's aw could.
Aw's get my wage — aw'm sure o' that;
He'll gi'e me o' ut's due,
An' mebbe, in His t'other place,
Some better wark to do.

Bu' then, aw reckon, 'tisn't th'stuff
We'n getten t'put i' th'loom,
Bu' what we mak' on't good or bad,
'Ut th'credit on't 'll come.
Some wark i' silk, an' other some
Ha'e cotton i' their gear;
Bu' silk or cotton matters nowt,
If nobbut th'skill be theere.

Bu' now it's nee' to th'end o' th'week,
An' close to th'reckonin' day:
Aw'll tak' my "piece" upon my back,
An' yer what th'Mester'll say:
An' if aw nobbut yer His voice
Pronounce my wark "weel done",
Aw'll straight forget o' th'trouble past
I' th'pleasure 'ut's begun.

A NOTE ON FEATHERED FRIENDS

Geoffrey Smerdon

IN OUR village every man over the age of reason kept pigeons and Billy Pickup was no exception. He was a quiet humourous man, a postman by day and a chimney sweep in the evenings; with a pink face and china-blue eyes which went well with his uniform; and it was a village mystery how he changed overnight from deepest grime to glowing spotlessnes. His wife Phoebe was (I thought privately) a witch- - - pear-shaped, grey-haired, ferret-faced with a single incisor at the front of her sharp mouth and a tongue which would take the varnish off a table. Her one virtue was cleanliness- - - and even this she contrived to make into a stick to beat poor gentle Billy's back. Patient soul that he was, he never rose to her provocation, but with a fine sense of irony invariably called her "my old geranium". Their family had all married spouses from other villages, no doubt leaving the rigours of Fern Cottage behind with a sigh of relief. Billy had no such escape, and was bullied year after year without a word of complaint.

Every evening when he came home to his tea- - - a sketchy affair as a rule- - - he was made to take his boots off in the porch and shuffle into the room in his stockinged feet, while Phoebe kept up an *obligato* of reproach which she had been storing up all day. Sometimes he escaped to his chimney sweeping, but when trade was slack he ate his sad portion in silence, put on his cap, and sidled down the yard in his slippers to the pigeon loft,. There he would sit for an hour or two smoking his pipe and meditating to a gentler accompaniment than Phoebe's nattering.

The pigeons were indeed Billy's pride and joy, though they were not a very distinguished flock and had been collected, piecemeal, by borrowings and dealings with his friends, exactly as Phoebe had stocked her garden. But his lifelong ambition was to own a pair of champions, a couple like the noble brutes that graced the cotes of his neighbour and crony, Alderman Sam Hothersall. It was a distant dream- - - like visiting Samarkand- - - but it lit Billy's daily path, and you never knew. The hard fact was though, that birds like that cost money and money did not drop through letter-boxes, nor for that matter down chimneys, as Billy knew only too well.

As the years went by and Phoebe's tongue was honed sharper and sharper, he took to having a quiet gill of Mild at the "Cock and Bottle" on his way home of an evening -- at least it postponed the inevitable moment of battle. There, over Mrs. Iddon's bar, he met his friends, all men of the fancy, and each as knowledgeable as the Editor of "Feathered World" himself. Sometimes in a mood of gay abandon he called for, or was bought a second gill, and when he got home found his tea an even less-than-usually-appetising ruin. On such days of course Phoebe's manner had even less treacle and even more brimstone in it.

One Friday late in December, however, was a red-letter day, for Billy found at the "Cock" that he had won a bottle of whiskey and two five-pound notes in the Christmas Draw. Flushed with a double ration of ale and the even headier wine of success, he poured out whiskey for the assembled company and, as bold as brass, bid a fiver each for two of Sam Hothersall's paragons that had recently had their pictures in the paper. Sam, full of bonhomie, took his bid, stumbled off to the lofts, and came back with the birds in a wicker basket which he plonked down on the bar. Billy was very late home that evening and Phoebe blazed away like a repeating rifle, but nothing could dim the glory of his triumph--- he felt as if he were leading in a Derby winner. But he kept his counsel and didn't mention the whiskey or the birds (which in fact he had already stowed safely away in the loft before he came in). Nevertheless he ate his devastated cottage-pie with quiet satisfaction and went to bed happy.

A week or two later, after a tiring wet day on his postman's round , Billy came home to find Phoebe mysteriously different. For one thing she had her best pinafore on instead of her usual sacking apron, and, even more unusual, she was smiling brightly and seemed actually pleased to see him.

They exchanged a few pleasantries and she retired to the kitchen and brought out his tea. Instead of the usual burnt offering, she laid on the table a large and noble pie, crisp-crusted, steaming and delicious, a dish of floury potatoes, a bowl of pink rhubarb and a jug of custard. "Yo look clemmed, lad," she said, "and Ah've med yo summat special toneet - - - summat right tasty." Amazed and drooling, Billy drew up his chair and set briskly to work on the pie. Phoebe, still beaming, sat in a rocking-chair and watched him. In next to no time he was mopping up the delicious gravy with a piece of bread and girding up his loins for a go at the rhubarb. But as he began to spoon it on to his plate, Phoebe reached out and touched his arm.

"Didst like it, lad?" she cooed, with a coy smile he hadn't seen in years.

"Champion, lass, ah've not etten a pie like yond since last Preston Guild- - - ah could manage one of them sort seven nights a week with no trouble at all."

"Could yo though," Phoebe answered, still smiling. "Could yo really?"

"Aye, ah could that!"

And in a flash Phoebe's winning smile changed to a snarl of triumph.

"Well yo couldn't, yo silly old begger," she cackled. "Yo couldn't afford it - - - not at ten pound a bloody go, yo couldn't!" - - - and with a burst of laughter like a machine-gun she stalked out into the kitchen in triumph.

Billy wept; and for a long time sat gazing into the fire. He was quieter and more patient than ever after that, but he still dreams about having two champions with their photos in the paper. He's lost his appetite for pies though.

BOWTON'S YARD

Samuel Laycock (1826-1893)

At number one, i' Bowton's Yard, mi gronny keeps a skoo,
Hoo hasna' mony scholars yet, hoo's nobbut one or two;
They sen th'owd woman's rayther cross — well, well it may be
    so;
Aw know hoo boxed me rarely once, an' poo'd mi ears an' o.

At number two lives widow Burns, hoo weshes clooas for folk;
The'r Billy, that's her son, gets jobs at wheelin' coke ;
They sen hoo cooarts wi' Sam-o'-Ned's, 'at lives at number
    three;
It may be so, aw conno tell, it matters nowt to me.

At number three, reet facin' th'pump, Ned Grimshaw keeps a
    shop;
He's Eccles-cakes, an' gingerbread, an' traycle beer an' pop;
He sells oat-cakes an' o, does Ned, he 'as boath soft an' hard,
An' everybody buys off him 'at lives i' Bowton's Yard.

At number four Jack Blunderick lives; he goes to th'mill an'
    wayves;
An' then, at th'weekend, when he's time, he pows a bit an'
    shaves;
He's badly off, is Jack, poor lad! he's rayther lawm, they
    sen,
An' his childer keep his deawn a bit, aw think they'n nine or
    ten.

At number five aw live misel', wi' owd Susannah Grimes,
But dunno like so very weel, hoo turns me eawt sometimes;
An' when aw'm in ther's ne'er no leet, aw have to ceawer i'
    th'dark;
Aw conno pay mi lodgin' brass becose aw'm eawt o' wark.

At number six, next door to us, an' close to th'side o'
    th'speawt,
Owd Susie Collins sells smo' drink, but hoo's welly allus
    beawt;
An' heaw it is, ut that is so, aw'm sure aw conno tell,

Hoo happen mak's it very sweet, 'an sups it o hersel!

At number seven ther's nob'dy lives, they laft it yesterday,
Th'bum baylis coom an' marked the'r things,an' took 'em o
away;
They took 'em in a donkey cart — aw know nowt wheer they
went —
Aw reckon they've bin ta'en an' sowd becose they owed some
rent.

At number eight — they're Yorkshire folk — ther's only th'mon
an' th'wife,
Aw think aw ne'er seed nicer folk nor these i' o mi loife!
Yo'll never see 'em foin' eawt, loike lots o' married folk,
They allus seem good-temper't like, an' ready wi a joke.

At number nine th'owd cobbler lives, th'owd chap ut mends mi
shoon,
He's gettin' very wake an' done, he'll ha' to leeov us soon;
He reads his Bible every day, an' sings just like a lark,
He says he's practisin for heaven — he's welly done his wark.

At number ten James Bowton lives, he's th'noicest heawse i'
th'row;
He's allus plenty o' summat t'ate, an' lots o' brass an' o;
An' when he rides or walks abeawt he's dressed up very fine,
But he isn't hawve as near to heaven as him at number nine.

At number 'leven mi uncle lives, aw co him Uncle Tum,
He goes to concerts up an' deawn, an' plays a kettle-drum;
I' bands o' music, an' sich things, he seems to tak' a pride,
An' allus mak's as big a noise as o i' th'place beside.

At number twelve, an' th'end o' th'row, Joe Stigging deols i'
ale;
He's sixpenny, an' fourpenny, dark-colour't, an' he's pale;
But aw ne'er touch it, for aw know it's ruin't mony a bard,
Aw'm th'only chap as doesn't drink 'at lives i' Bowton's Yard!

An' neaw aw've done, aw'll say goodbye, an' leeov yo' for a
while;
Aw know aw haven't towd mi tale i' sich a fust-rate style;
But iv yo're pleas't aw'm satisfied, an' ax for no reward
For tellin' who mi neighbours are ut live i' Bowton's Yard.

THE WISEST DOG IN THE WORLD

Eric Halsall

RACING out over this wild snow covered Pennine Moor, the collie dog goes to its task of gathering the hill, bringing in the sheep to its master who crouches for shelter from the screaming wind behind the grey stone wall.

Whilst in sight the dog is able to be directed and commanded by the whistles of the shepherd; when it goes from sight over the moor top it is on its own. The collie does not falter when the whistled instructions cease. It knows its job, it is wise in the ways of sheep and knows where they will be lying in shelter from the snow.

The dog races on, casting out in a wide sweep of the moor so that every sheep it raises will move inwards to form an ever-growing flock in the centre of the dog's run. It bends further out to cover sheep which appear on the near horizon of the rough hags of moorland: it runs fast, faltering only when deep wind-blown snow makes progress difficult. It flounders through the drifts, runs over the short bents, leaps the narrow water gullies, and carefully picks its way over soft peat, knowing the moor as well as the sheep themselves.

The wind buffets, flinging icy snow-flakes, cutting the collie's long coat to a knife-edge parting. Over a mile from its master in this bleakest of terrains, the dog works entirely on its own initiative, turning the sheep on their way, and when having completed its encirclement of the flock on this section of the hill, coming in behind them to drive them to its master.

It is a feat of shepherding that makes man wonder at the intelligence of the humble collie dog. Yet it is commonplace, an every-day happening on these Pennine hills. Whenever the flock has to be gathered- - - for vetting, for counting, for clipping, for dipping, for putting to the tup, or as on this day just to check that none is snowbound and to bring them nearer home in the bad weather- - - it is the collie dog that does the work.

No man can say with certainty who taught the first dog the art of herding sheep, or from what dim roots the first sheepdog sprang. They are among the oldest of domestic dogs, the first friend of primitive man. Aeons before Christ, the Shepherd of

Man, walked among the sheep flocks on the hills above Galilee, there were sheepdogs guarding the flocks of man.

Down the centuries, and particularly in the last half-century, man has improved the working collie by selective breeding, and today the modern sheepdog- - - the Border Collie- - - is medium sized, light on its feet, compact, fast as the wind, of a dominant mind in stock mastery, and supremely intelligent- - - the wisest dog in the world.

* * * * * *

The twins are stranded. Tiny, woolly coated helpless lambs- - - one sooty black faced, the other black and white faced- - - stand, bleating pathetically, on the bank of the River Brun.

Across the water their mother ewe calls commandingly for them to join her. But between mother and youngsters is a racing barrier of cold leaping water. Earlier in the day, the ewe had led her twins across the water to graze on the opposite bank of the river. Since then, in a matter of hours, heavy rain on the hills of Black Hameldon had poured water into the source of the river and the downstream level had risen.

Now the ewe has recrossed the Brun, but the twins have faltered before the racing waters, which are more terrifying in appearance than in depth. Stubbornly, the ewe will not return to her lambs. She nibbles the grass, lifts her head, twitches her ears to their pathetic bleats- - -and calls on them to join her. When Meg, the little collie, hears their bleats, the twins have been tottering on the brink of indecision and the river for ten minutes, one moment moving forward with the intention to brave the waters, the next ranging the bank for an easier crossing, the while calling their plight to their parent- - - who still acts heedless of their cries.

The little collie, familiar with the ways of the sheep on the farm, interprets their calls of fear, and trots across the field towards them, disturbing a strong buck rabbit on her way.

She spurns the chase, and moves up towards the lambs who, seeing her, momentarily cease their noise, and then with renewed vigour call their plight to their mother. Showing some signs of protective instinct at last, the ewe moves down the opposite bank, but she does not enter the water.

Meg moves quietly up on the lambs, and her steady and purposeful approach holds them. They try to run upstream, but the collie glides round to head them. They start to dash downstream, but the dog is there again to cut them off. There is only one course open to them. They jump into the river, and in two bounds gain the opposite bank, unharmed and only a little wet. Suddenly safe and contented, they seek their mother's udder and suck milk- - - their little adventure over.

A cynical magpie which has watched the whole incident from the bough of an alder chatters scorn on the stupid ways of sheep, and Meg goes back to seek the rabbit in the field.

MISS MEREDITH

Malcolm Dockeray

*(Being reflections upon a Lancashire school in the
1930's)*

She stands before us
At her desk.
Poor soul, trying so hard to give her best;
The high flush on cheek and neck
It comes and goes so rapidly
As she wages that everlasting strife
In vain to hide that change in life.

A gallant show she makes standing there
With carefully bleached yellow hair.
We children sit gazing open-mouthed
As once a week the history lesson comes round.

"Archery", announces Miss Meredith
"Is what Queen Elizabeth liked the best."
And really we children can honestly swear
That we can see the great Eliza standing there
As Miss Meredith strikes her stately pose
With a large imaginary bow and arrows.
She speaks with such authority
I'm sure she knew Elizabeth. . . personally.

Similarly, scripture is her metier. . .
And certainly Miss Meredith seems to know
All about heaven.
Perhaps she has made the journey recently
And carefully briefed that unknown territory.

"Heaven's a wonderful place," says she
With her odd and jerky way of speech.
"It's summer there all the year round
And waterfalls and such scenery
As we never have in our country."

We children sit with eyes wide and glistening;
There are delighted whisperings
Throughout the class,
For we can see Miss Meredith, flying high
To those lovely mansions in the sky- - -
Her angel wings and harp are there,
A halo above her golden hair.
And all the lesser angelic souls
Sing her welcome in tuneful tones.

"But," says she, with hand aloft,
The watery eyes go suddenly dark,
"The road there is difficult,
A pathway stony, hard and rough.
Though," here an indifferent shrug,
"If we've led a good life
We needn't be afraid.
King George the Fifth,"
Here her voice is raised
In patriotic fervour,
"When he dies
He won't be afraid
To walk that path
So difficult and dangerous."

Bless you, dear Miss Meredith.
You made a heaven on earth
For us.

FETTLER

Edith Collison

THERE'S an owd chap i' eawr village as foak co' "Fettler". T'name suits him, fer he'll tackle ver'near owt wo'th fettlin' — a bed-leg through t'ceilin', rainin'-in, a watch i' bits. He's getten an urge fer settin' things reet. There's nobbut one job as he'll ne'er tackle — fettlin' a trap fer catchin' a wild thing.

"Not wi' these hands," he'll say.

When Johnny Balshaw's hen-cabin went o'er t'pasture hillock i' a gale, an' wur smasht up, Fettler fotcht t'pieces back, an' put that shed i' bet'ther shape nor it hed bin fer monny a while. Johnny Balshaw wurn't th' only un as wur suited, fer t'cock crowed aw day, an' went i'side monny a time, it wur that set-up wi t'place.

Sally Jump hes but one lad, an' when he geet his yed stuck i' a pon, his mam couldn't shift t'little sowjer's helmet. T'lad wur skrikin' summat awfu', Sally wur ver'near eawt o' her wits, an' t'neebours wur stonnin' in t'dooar-hole, doin' nowt, when Fettler come by. He shoved t'wimmen aside an' went in.

"It's mi best pon," Sally cries.

"Aye, an' it's thi best lad, think on," ses Fettler, reytchin' fer a feather an' th'oil-can eawt o' his bass, an' i'two ticks, t'little lad wur i' dayleet agen.

Then there wur a do wi' Parson's shoon. One Sunda' morn, after service, Fettler hung abeawt till Parson come eawt. "Excuse me, sir," ses Fettler, "but if you'll let me hev them shoon to'morn, Ah'll fettle 'em." Parson wur flummoxt. He'd on'y just bowt 'em, he sed. "Aye," ses Fettler, "Ah thowt so. They've getten a squeak. Ah'll shift it if yo'll let me." Parson let him.

Fettler loves trees, an' when t'Squire hed th'owd beech tree done away wi', Fettler ne'er went near t'place fer monny a while — sed as it wur like loisin' a friend, an' summat bonny hed gone. Squire an' Fettler get on weel together. Squire thinks as Fettler's a grand chap, deawn to earth — nay, t'saut on it.

Once, when Squire wur took bad, Fettler went a-seein' him. He wur i' bed, an' poorly-lookin'. Squire towd him as he thowt his time hed come, he felt that bad, an' he shut his een. Aw at once he oppent 'em, managed a bit of a smile, an' towd Fettler as this wur summat he couldn't ax him to fettle. Th'owd chap fillt up, he wur that upset.

"Nay, sir," he ses. "Ah'll fotch Parson, an' he'll ax t'Chief Fettler to mek thee bet'ther."

It wur a long do, afore Squire wur on his feet agen.

Fettler hes a lad i' foreign parts, an' a lass, Young Bet (fifty if hoo's a day). Hoo lives nearby, an' if her dad'll let her, hoo does bits o' things fer him. But he hes his pride. Once, when hoo swisht a fly off t'clooas on t'rack, hoo slipt off a buffet an' rickt her ankle.

"Sithee, lass," he towd her. "Ah con manage. Ah'm not that owd. Think on, Ah'm done if tha does fer me."

If yo' ax Fettler what a job'll cost, he allus ses, "Stuff an' time." Foak as are near wi' their brass pays that, but if times are bad wi' yo, he'll tek just fer t'stuff.

When he wur a lad, Fettler served his time to joinerin' at four bob a week, wi' ninepence eawt fer "tool-money". He's still getten t'same hommer as he knockt his fust nail in wi'. "It went in awreet," he'll tell yo wi' a laugh, "but th'end come eawt next dooer an' t'boss sent me to shove t'nail back!"

He tells tales o' leg-pullin' he hed, an' th'errands he went fer silly tackle, like elbow-grease, a rubber hommer, an' a left-honded screw-driver. T'best do wur bein' sent fer summat co'ed "Gumguachem". He wur a serious lad, anxious to please, an' he kept sayin' t'word aw t'way to t'shop, but when he landed, he'd lost it. T'chap i' t'shop knew what gam'wur hed wi' new lads.

"Try an' say it," he tells Fettler.

"Two pennorth o'---o'---please sir, it seawnds like 'By gum go at 'em."

T'chap med up a little parcel, took t'brass, an' back went Fettler.

"Well?" axes foremon.

"Ah've got it!" ses t'lad, an' gi'es him t'parcel.

Dost know what wur in it? Some o' them sweets as they co'ed 'Cupid's Whispers'!

T'joiners roared, but t'foremon wur mad. He wurn't wed---not even in t'walkin' eawt stage — an' it wur his tuppence!

Fettler's owd neaw, an' gettin' t'ords th'end, but he keeps his tools ready. Foak gi'e him bits o' jobs, an' yo should see t'joy on his face as he does 'em. It meeans summat when yo're owd to

164

feel as yo're still wanted. Someday we'll hev to do beawt him, but Ah bet when he gooes, if he hes his way, there'll be a bit o' fettlin' an' oilin' fer him in t'next world!

Owd champion! We'll miss thi busy fingers an' thi kind heart!

CONVERSATION

Burton Grainger (written 1956)

WHAT'S id all like now, lad, and me welly fifteen years deep? "Chimneys grow best in the sooty fields, grandad, and the coltsfoot slag-hills by the railway side. The old loved walks still and the little black train with trucks of clinkers buffets the quarries under Hamilton Hill. But they've lately built a works for cement and a little red town that looks bombed with a monster bag of flour. And there's a pale field at the back and dusty trees for the kids to climb."

"Where, lad, where's t'little red, dusty town?"

"Oh away past your cemetery's garden of granite. And there's new flats too, like little stacked bungalows with verandahs, by the bus-stop where we went back once because grandma lost her wheezy chest's blue-glass brooch, and I knew where and never told her."

"Aye, I remember. Why didn't ta tell her, lad?"

"I was too shy and there were people in best black clothes."

"Tha were allus backwards at coming forwards. Thi father were t'same, poor lad. But grandma'd enough of sorrow thad day, and thi mother, widowed to a shadow."

"I'm sorry, grandad."

"What's sorry now, lad. Is it still the same old town?"

"From the blessing of the little hills you can still see its stony garden, weedy with assorted chimney stacks rolling their smoke, same old spire-cluttered, foundry-choked, smothering town and the intricate maze of black and breathing avenues of little homes. Still the old smouldering town, making mangles and cotton, machines, disinfectant and toffee, muck and money."

"Who runs id now? Is Councillor Robinson still knocking about?"

"Robinson?"

"Ben Robinson, and Charlie Livesey as married Jenny Thorpe, and owd Ball as collected ground-rents for our Riley Terrace?"

"All gone, grandad. But I remember them well. Mr. Ball who sat with his Chinese old hand on his wavering stick and the near-blind old sheepdog with one blue eye, and Mr. Livesey, and Ben Robinson, bow-legged as a hoop. All double watch-chain men with waistcoats and boots, watching the young men bowl with those liquorice mats on Buller Park green. Slow wonderful men with the town on their hearts."

"Aye, grand owd chaps. And what become of my garden on Riley's row?"

"It never coloured again. They kept your brown-splashed rockery glinting with pearl. But a young man who hadn't the garden love when he stooped couldn't grow things. He hadn't your thumbs."

"Ay never say thad, as my garden's gone.

"When you bent slow with your big man's body, high in that terrace garden, scarce as big as a room, when your boots creaked reaching for earwigs on match-boxed sticks, when you stood up red-faced with a few plucked lazy plants for the fire-back, you could see that garden grow. Lupins like blue pagodas and dahlias as big as your head. And the roses went up the trellis like serpents with red in their mouths."

"I loved thad garden. And women as passed said how lovely id were. . ."

"And listened to your stories, told with whiskery plants in your earthy hands. No, the garden's gone now, and the house looks strange, and the gate wants paint."

"Is Buller's foundry still working, lad?"

"Buller's is still the town. And the red fire in its square hole of hell with sparks, and shirt-sleeved men passing by. The iron trucks that tip to one wheel, full of ingots like logs. The little office box dusty-brown and windows greased with grey, and a mucky clerk with ink-pots stuck with pens. And the great four-storey machine-busy mansion with thousands of smoking windows as if it were taking fire. And the dim like a barrier across the street all blue with the smell of hot iron. Buller's is still the town. Black streets like canyons, with black walls and a strip of the sky. Black streets with managers' dozing cars, and overalled men walking with shouldered, see-sawing strips, and men shoving trucks like pushing down walls. Lorries with cylinders like colossal save-alls, and a crane with a fish-hook big enough for a whale."

"And at a quarter-past-five the black-faced men coming out. First the crippled men who jerk on their one good leg. Then the dam-burst of men and apprentice lads, with their bait-tins, running half into the street with their arms out to balance, all smelling of oil-smell and rust. Still the same at quarter past-five with the street in a flood, like a dirty flood of men in revolt marching fast down the centre of the road. And buses and cars in their midst going slow because the men are too many for danger and won't give way. And then when the men have cleared, the doors standing open dusty into the street, and a strange quiet like Sunday, and the foundry waiting warm for the night-shift to come."

"Aye, I can smell it, lad, hear t'slap of beltings afore t'machines were knocked on. And what's factory bottom like? Tell me, lad."

"Three great chimneys, armfuls for giants, that polish up fine when it rains, and the old lodge, and the railway, and three old mills. Still the old clattering doorway and threads in the gutter, and smell of coarse cotton and heat. And little tackler men with downy-white aprons and bloom on their caps like flour. Yards full of cobbles and baskets stamped with black numbers.

"At half-past five, still the women with clogs and pint pots. And they come out all talking as if they had gone in so and ended it now. Black-stockings and clogs that clack on the pavements, and girls laughing and swinging thin streams of tea-leaves out of their pots across the drain in the gutter, and then lifting their black legs to pick thread off their shins. Women walking home without looking, in clumps, talking and shrieking, and stopping to howl."

"That's id, lad, that's th'owd town. . ."

"And at home in the houses iron smell and cotton smell meeting; houses little and old, with backyards and clattering ash-bins, and slamming of lavatory doors. Low walls and cats on the spikes of glass. Then the paper-lad shouting and crossing the garden fronts, throwing in the news at the little vestibules. And the club-man bursting straight in with his book to pick up shillings off the dresser-end."

"Aye lad, I remember id all. . . . ."

LANCASHIRE ENGLISH

By kind permission of The Burnley Express

TEST your understanding of the language spoken by some of the local people: this is a valuable introduction to a Southerner coming up North for the first time, and for student teachers trying to understand how their pupils communicate with each other.

(Translate the "g" as in "got")

1. Intitot?
2. Giuzit
3. Summat supoereor
4. Gerritetten
5. Geroffit.
6. Supwithee?
7. Smarerweeim?
8. Iampgorrit.
9. Azzeeginiter?
10. Esmiatonreet?
11. Eez gooinooam.
12. Asta gorrit reight?
13. Isit themum?
14. Asta gorrit withy?
15. Purrimineer.
16. Ayampt eared nowt.
17. Thafta gerra newun.
18. Eesezitintiz---burra berritiz.
19. Lerrus gerrus answesht.
20. Summonemz gorragerroff ·
21. Wiv gorra gerruz imbux
22. Thamun gerrit lernt.
23. Shut thigob.
24. Owzeeno?
25. Aberritinterz.
26. Comforrus arpastate itmornin.
27. Nardendenn watardooin?
28. Asta seenim ontelly?
29. It dunt marrer.
30. Lerrus gurrat pixchers.
31. Asta gorratanner?
32. Eenose nowtabartit.
33. Eez gonna gerrit.
34. Lerrer gerontbus.
35. Eedurnt purrized unert watter.
36. Eesezeeantadit.
37. Oowurriwee?
38. Ateldim burrewontlissen.
39. Lerim purrizaton.
40. Ostle clowt thee ifta duntgioor.
41. Tinintin.
42. Gerary tergithi an and wieet.
43. Eez gorriz atoam.
44. Thawantsta weshhi eeroll aht.
45. Thakkon iftha wants.
46. Wivgorracar.
47. Eez nobbuta babbi.
48. Tantad nowt dunnatitas I knows on.
49. Cantha kumter owerowse tunneet?
50. Weezt gaffer?

Marking:

10 correct answers:	You are obviously an immigrant from the south.
25 correct answers:	You are on your way to becoming a settler.
40 correct answers:	You have settled.
All answers correct:	Tha wantsta brush up on thi Queen's English.

* Not to be confused with Lancashire *Dialect!* (ED)

T'BAND I' T'PARK

Hilda Hamer

"BOB, dusti remember eawh we first met? Ah ust t' like gooain' t'park, when t'band played on a Sunday afternoon."

"Aye, tha looked real bonny! Tha'd a blue frock on, an' a white hat, an' thi een wer' as blue as thi frock an' t'sky that bonny day."

"Get away wi' thi, mi hat wer' pale pink! Tha ne'er could tell one colour fro' another."

"Id wer' white! Ah owt t'know, wern't id mi birthday?"

"Ah dooant think tha towd mi that. An' what had that got t'do wi' t'colour o' mi hat? Gawmless!"

"Ah'll just fill t'coil bucket an mek t'fire up, then Ah'll be off to t'park. Tha'll be awreight, weant ti?"

As Bob went eawt o' t'room Hannah lay back on her spotless white pillows an' allowed memories t'flow areawnd her. When hoo'd bin a lass, hoo'd loved t'walk i' t'park afther Sunday Schoo', but t'Sundays when t'band played wer' red-letter days, fer hoo loved music. Besides, there wer' allus plenty o' boys an' girls t'talk to. T'sun an' t' fleawrs shone, t'swans on t'lake sailed majestically by, t'ducks quacked, an' t'babbies i' their smart prams crowed. Oh! it wer' such a perfect day when hoo met Bob! Eighteen year owd, hoo felt like a queen i' her blue dress—an' Bob wer' so handsome; small-boned, wi' flashin' breawn een! Did they flash fer her? It wer' months after when hoo knew they did!

Neaw here hoo wer', bedfast, an' Bob hed t'gooa to t'park wi'eawt her . . .Victoria Park ud be lovely today. T'roses ud be i' bloom, it'd be lovely t'sit i' a deck-chair ageean i' t'sun. . . No deck-chairs fer t'lads an' lasses when hoo used t'gooa wi' her friend to t'band; t'grass wer' good enough to sit on i' those days. . . .Ah don't suppose Ah could even get so far deawn neaw, sin' Ah hed this arthritis i' mi knees, thowt Hannah, but Ah'd like t'yer t'band!

"Tha'll be awreight, lass, fer an heawr or two, Ah've put some orange-juice i' t'feedin'-cup theer, an' here's thi book. Ah'll be off neaw. Ah'll be back t'mek thi tay."

"Ah'll be awreight, lad, tha needn't hurry back. Hasti some money fer t'collection? An' remember Ah want t'know all abeawt id when tha comes hooam!"

"Stop thi worritin', Ah'll tell thi all abeawt it!"

Bob bent deawn an' gave Hannah a kiss, an' started eawt fer t'park. Two heawrs later he coom hooam t'find Hannah full o' pain, an' his recital of events hed t'be postponed.

T' next mornin' Hannah wer' better, an' Bob wer' that suited---after he'd med t'breakfast he sat deawn an' towd his tale. Although he thowt he'd med it as breet as he could, Hannah didn't seem amused. He thowt hoo mun be sleepy still, fer t'tales o' t'band hed allus reawsed her bifoore. . .

It wern't t'same as when Hannah an' he used t'gooa theer, theawsands used t'turn up. Yesterday he'd bi surprised if there wer' mooar ner a hundred theer. There wer' a time when wi couldn't move along t'paths fer fooak stoppin' fer a few words, he thowt. . .Good owd days thi wer'! T'military bands played Colonel Bogey an' Gilbert an' Sullivan. It wer' allus gay an' lively. Neaw thi played nowt but beat music, "Yeah, yeah, yeah"---heaw daft could thi get? No! Life weren't as breet wi'eawt Hannah t'walk an' talk wi'. Bob thowt he wouldn't dress up agen t'yer t'band i' t'park; even t'fleawrs wern't as nice wi'eawt her.

"Get th'owd concertina eawt, Bob, an' play us a tune. Ah'd like t'yer some o' th'owd songs. Play t'Galloping Major, an' Ah'm off to Philadelphia, like tha used to. Mi fahther used t'sing 'em an' aw."

"What, at ten o'clock i't'mornin'! Tha'll ha' t'neighbours talkin'!"

"Ne'er mind t'neighbours. Ah'd like th'owd tunes onytime."

"Awreight, lass, thi wer' gradely tunes."

Bob went upstairs an' dug th'owd concertina eawt o't'bottom o' t'wardrobe, but when he sat deawn bi t'bed-side Hannah wer' asleep. He started fiddlin' abeawt wi' t'kehs as quiet as he could, fer he'd forgotten all he ever knew abeawt it, it wer' that long sin' he'd hed howd o' it. As it gave a sudden groan he glanced at his wife's face, an' realised Hannah would never yer him play t'concertina ageean. Hoo'd gone t'yer t'band i' t'park bi hersel'.

172

JUMPIN' JACK

Eric Holt

Watch 'im goo, you gradely prancer,
Tappin' toes, an' clackin' 'eels;
Jumpin' Jack, 'ee's best clug dancer
E'er stepped eawt wi' jigs an' reels.

Twistin', turnin', pointin', prancin',
While th'owd fiddle sings away;
Leeter than a fither dancin'
On a breeze i' t'month o' May.

Watch yon childer clap together,
Keepin' time to t'click an' clack;
Summer, winter, onny weather,
Eawt they coom to Jumpin' Jack.

Carnivals corn't do wi 'eawt 'im,
Churches want 'im fer t'bazaars;
Ower-Sixties weren't bi beawt 'im,
Sooner 'im than t'Telly stars.

Pair on pair o' clugs 'ee's batthered,
Still 'is pins er straight an' true
As on t'day when fust 'ee clatthered
I' new clogs when 'ee were two.

Jack, lad, keep thi toes i' fettle,
Make eawr spirits gay an' leet.
Tho' thi clugs er shod wi' metal—
Wi find gowd i' them two feet!

WITCHCRAFT IN PENDLE FOREST

Harrison Ainsworth (1592-1638)
(from 'The Lancashire Witches')

DESCENDING the hill, and passing through the thicket, the party came within a short distance of Goldshaw Booth, when they were met by a cowherd, who, with looks of great alarm, told them that John Law, the pedlar, had fallen down in a fit in the clough, and would perish if they did not stay to help him. As the poor man in question was well known both to Nicholas and Roger Nowell, they immediately agreed to go to his assistance, and accompanied the cowherd along a bye-road which led through the clough to the village.

They had not gone far when they heard loud groans, and presently afterwards found the unfortunate pedlar lying on his back, and writhing in agony. He was a large, powerfully-built man of middle age, and had been in the full enjoyment of health and vigour, so that his sudden prostration was the more terrible.

His face was greatly disfigured, the mouth and neck drawn awry, the left eye pulled down, and the whole power of the same side gone.

"Why, John, this is a bad business," cried Nicholas. "You have had a paralytic stroke, I fear."

"Nah---Nah---squoire," replied the sufferer, speaking with difficulty, "it's neaw nat'ral ailment, it's witchcraft."

"Witchcraft!" exclaimed Potts, who had come up, and producing his memorandum-book. "Another case. Your name and description, friend?"

"John Law o' Cown, pedlar," replied the man.

"John Law of Colne, I suppose, petty chapman," said Potts, making an entry. "Now, John, my good man, be pleased to tell us by whom you have been bewitched"

"By Mother Demdyke," groaned the man.

"Mother Demdyke---ah!" exclaimed Potts. "Good, very good! Now, John, as to the cause of your quarrel with the old hag?"

"Ey con scarcely rekillect it, my head be so confused, mester," replied the pedlar.

"Make an effort, John," persisted Potts, "it is most desirable such a dreadful offender should not escape justice."

"Weel, weel, ey'n try an' tell it, then," replied the pedlar. "Yo mun knoa ey wur crossing the hill fro' Cown to Rough Lee, wi'

174

my pack upon my shouthers, when who should ey meet boh Mother Demdyke, an' hoo axt me to gi' her some scithers an' pins, boh, os ill luck wad ha' it, ey refused."

"Yo had better do it, John," hoo said, "or yo'll rue it efore to-morrow neet."

Ey laughed at her, an' trudged on, boh when I looked back, and seed her shakin' her skinny hond at me, ey repented and thowt ey would go back, an' gi' her the choice o' my wares. Boh my pride wur too strong, an' ey walked on to Barley an' Ogden, an' slept at Bess's o' th'Booth, an' woke this mornin' stout and strong, fully persuaded th' owd witch's threat would come to nowt. Alack-a-day! ey wur out i' my reckonin', fo' scarcely had ey reached this kloof, o'my way to Sabden, than ey wur seized wi' a sudden shock, os if a thunder-bowt had hit me, an' ey lost the use o' my lower limbs, an' t'laft soide, an' should ha' deed most likely, if it hadna been fo' Ebil o' Jem's o' Dan's, who spied me out, an' brought me help."

"Yours is a deplorable case indeed, John," said Richard, "especially if it be the result of witchcraft."

"You do not surely doubt that it is so, Master Richard?" cried Potts.

"I offer no opinion," replied the young man; "but a paralytic stroke would produce the same effect. But instead of discussing the matter, the best thing we can do will be to transport the poor man to Bess's o' th'Booth, where he can be attended to."

"Tom and I can carry hem there if Abel will take charge of his pack," said one of the grooms.

"That I win," replied the cowherd unstrapping the box, upon which the sufferer's head rested, and placing it on his own shoulders.

Meanwhile a gate having been taken from its hinges by Sparshot and the reeve, the poor pedlar, who groaned deeply during the operation, was placed upon it by the men, and borne towards the village, followed by the others, leading their horses.

Great consternation was occasioned in Goldshaw Booth by the entrance of the cavalcade, and still more when it became known that John Law, the pedlar, who was a favourite with all, had had a frightful seizure. Old and young flocked forth to see him, and the former shook their heads, while the latter were appalled at the hideous sight.

Master Potts took care to tell them that the poor fellow was bewitched by Mother Demdyke, but the information failed to produce the effect he anticipated, and served rather to repress than heighten their sympathy for the sufferer. The attorney concluded, and justly, that they were afraid of incurring the displeasure of the vindictive old hag by an open expression of interest in his fate.

So strongly did this feeling operate that, after bestowing a glance of commiseration at the pedlar, most of them returned, without a word, to their dwellings. On their way to the little hostel whither they were conveying the poor pedlar, the party passed the church, and the sexton, who was digging a grave in the yard, came forward to look at them, but on seeing John Law, he seemed to understand what had happened, and resumed his employment.

A wide-spreading yew tree grew in this part of the church-yard, and near it stood a small cross rudely carved in granite, marking the spot where, in the reign of Henry V1., Ralph Cliderhow, tenth Abbot of Whalley, held a meeting of the tenantry to check encroachments.

Not far from this ancient cross the sexton, a hale old man, with a fresh complexion and silvery hair, was at work, and while the others went on, Master Potts paused to say a word to him.

"You have a funeral here to-day, I suppose, Master Sexton?" he said.

"Yeigh," replied the man, gruffly.

"One of the villagers?" inquired the attorney.

"Neaw; hoo were na o' Goldshey," replied the sexton.

"Where then---who was it?" persevered Potts.

The sexton seemed disinclined to answer, but at length said, "Meary Baldwyn, the miller's dowter o' Rough Lee, os protty a lass os ever yo see, mester. Hoo wur the apple o' her feyther's ee, an' he hasna had a dry ee sin hoo deed. Wall-a-day! we mun aw go, awd an' young, an' protty Meary Baldwyn went young enough. Poor lass, poor lass!"

And he brushed the dew from his eyes with his brawny hand.

'Was her death sudden?" asked Potts.

"Neaw, not so sudden, mester" replied the sexton. "Ruchot Baldwyn had fair warnin'. Six months ago, Meary wur ta'en ill, an' fro' t'furst he knoad how it wad eend."

"How so, friend?" asked Potts, whose curiosity began to be aroused.

"Becose—" replied the sexton; and he stopped suddenly short.

"She was bewitched?" suggested Potts.

The sexton nodded his head, and began to ply his mattock vigorously.

"By Mother Demdyke?" inquired Potts, taking out his memorandum-book.

The sexton again nodded his head, but spake no word, and meeting some obstruction in the ground, took up his pick to remove it

"Another case!" muttered Potts, making an entry. "Mary Baldwyn, daughter of Richard Baldwyn, of Rough Lee, aged—How old was she, sexton?"

"Throtteen," replied the man; "boh dunna ax me ony more questions, mester. Th'berrin takes place i' an hour, and ey hanna half digged the grave."

"Your own name, Master Sexton, and I have done," said Potts.

"Zachariah Worms," answered the man.

"Worms—ha! an excellent name for a sexton," cried Potts. "You provide food for your family, eh, Zachariah?"

"Tut—tut," rejoined the sexton, testily; "go an' moind yer own business, mon, and leave me to moind mine."

"Very well, Zachariah," replied Potts.

And having obtained all he required, he proceeded to the little hostel, where, finding the rest of the party dismounted, he consigned Flint to a cowherd, and entered the house.

HEYSHAM HEAD – NOVEMBER SCENE

Frances Harland

Such colours as are constantly
used to describe the dreams of youth
lie to the west;
The sun between black clouds is slash of red
fit for a flag of love, fit for a banner
of a crusading and releasing war;
sand, and the still sea gleam
brass-bright or as molten steel from the furnace poured
glittering like a visionary path
beyond the green safe innocent fold of the fields;

    but turn, look to the north---
no hill's horizon, no cloud-height, no depth,
no land-mark and no buoys,
but out of the silent white
the tide creeps in like age.
Below, the treacherous rocks at the cliff foot
one by one are eaten without a sound
by this silk-lipped encroachment.
    So, turn to go;
    step carefully;
here the cliff's bent brow
keeps human sorrow shadowly held in stone;
here are the graves of yester-centuries---
the covering earth has long been swept away
dust unto sand returning to the sea---
the leaden lids are gone, and flesh within,
the bones laid level to the sun's last rays---
only the stone remains, in its grey curve
for head and shoulder and thigh, fashioned by Saxon hands,
holding the deeper grey of last night's rain.
Turn slowly, slowly now from cloud and sun—

    step carefully
    the last of light
throws your long shadow deeper in the dusk,
the dusk that creeps like the sea that creeps like age
that needs no voice to say
here ends the common current of all life.

OUR CUT

E. Josephine Penn

DURING a recent broadcast on the problems arising from the ever increasing noise and pollution of the 20th century, the speaker made the somewhat startling prediction that bicycles and canals would one day make a comeback. Since a branch of the Liverpool and Leeds canal runs parallel with the narrow lane in which I live, emptying itself via locks into the River Douglas, a mere two fields beyond my orchard, I have been fascinated by the idea, ruminating nostalgically on the past of this now semi-derelict waterway.

Tidal waters have always depressed and frightened me, whereas I can derive serenity and relaxation from a walk alongside a gently-moving canal. The one is, as it were, a wild beast ever ready to pounce and devour; while the other, though still a beast, since it does on occasion claim its victims, is a beast with its fangs drawn, a lazy benevolent creature, sheltering and sustaining plant and animal, and mild in the service of man.

No sooner was school over for the day than we children would be off to "The Cut"— in summer to swim or fish, in winter when the ice held, to slide and skate. It was our playground, our seaside, our nature reserve, and when we crossed either of its wooden foot-bridges we were, so to speak, in a foreign land, the parish of Hoole. There we collected tadpoles in the marsh pools, gathered mushrooms, or gazed at the house, now a dolls' museum, from whose window above the porch the great Jeremiah Horrocks, father of British astronomy, became the first man to observe the passage of Venus across the disc of the sun. His name, 330 years later, is still a household word in the district; he figures in the East window of the roadside church where he was once curate, and is immortalised by a tablet in Westminster Abbey.

The significance of the word "Cut", now rarely used, was brought home to me recently when an old gentleman, nearing 100, told me of how his grandfather had watched the building of this last mile of the branch. In the early 19th. century there were no mechanical wonders to slice through clay and stone like a knife through butter, only spades and barrows with which to cut the channel and raise the banks. Just below the bridge carrying the Preston road, now known as "Killer Bridge", stand substantial warehouses where cotton was once stored en route from Liverpool, and it is only quite recently that certain local houses acquired 'souvenir' walls after the demolition of the old Gunpowder House. This stone building stood further along the bank, and square-sail boats used to make the trip to Greenodd near Windermere with coal, bringing back lime, and gunpowder for use in the mines. All barrels containing the latter were made with copper nails, and the men moving them had to wear slippers, lest contact with iron should spark off disaster.

The old Lock-house, built by the man who endowed the local grammar school, now a Bank, still peers over a thicket of currant and gooseberry bushes, and the present lock-master can trace an unbroken family connection with the first occupant of the house. Behind this was once a cindered platform, complete with seat and oil-lamp, from which a little one-compartment train started its journey along the high bank of the Douglas, past wild bluebell woods to the main railway station. As passengers clung to their seats, its shrill whistle would scatter the birds and invite a toot from passing barges.

With the advent of buses, this quaint little rural service ceased to operate, and few people then could have possibly visualised the subsequent closure of the main line from Preston to Southport, turning this, and lanes like it, into veritable maelstroms. Articulated, and other heavy vehicles, thunder past at all hours, shaking houses, fraying nerves, and charging the atmosphere with attar of petrol. Since the entire track, together with stations and some bridges, was ruthlessly torn up as soon as the last train was withdrawn---in order that land might be developed---the one and only solution to the traffic problem is obviously the revitalisation of the canal. The nucleus of a boatyard has already sprung up on the west bank, near the locks, to meet the ever increasing interest in sailing; and here, from time to time, fabulous luxury yachts come up the Douglas for a face-lift, looking like exotic flowers scornfully surveying a wilderness of nettles and coarse grasses, from which the odd mooring-stump occasionally protrudes. Within shouting distance a modern engineering firm disturbs the silence, while industrial waste from a textile mill discourages both lily and coot. Three trends of a modern era alongside the ghost of a bygone fashion...

Anything carried to excess must, sooner or later, defeat and confound its own ends, a state of affairs to which our highly mechanised transport system is surely heading. It is neither intelligent, nor a good thing health-wise, to be continually dashing from A to B and at the greatest possible speed, being bored on the motorways and seeing nothing in the sky. Life was meant to be lived to the full, not just got over, and so it may well be that, in the not too distant future, that recent broadcast prophecy will come true, bringing a fresh boost to the cycle trade, renewed life to the inland waterways, and perhaps, who knows, some relief to the medical profession.

FOLK SONG '73

Al Potts

T'new Motorway's comin', there's nowt we con do!
Eawr heawse an' eawr street'll be riven i' two
So as aw them lung lorries an' cars con rush thro'---
    An' we're beawn to be flittin' i' t'mornin'.

It's months ago neaw sin' that fancy young chap
Come fro' t'Council to toak abeawt t'new Pennine Gap,
Well to us it wor nobbut a line on a map---
    But it's meant that we're flittin' in t'mornin'.

Mi uncle Tum's farmland they're sweeping away,
An' t'chip-shop on t'corner, an' t'Chapel, they say;
In a bit there'll be nowt but bulldozers an' clay
    Wheer we clatthered to t'Mill of a mornin'.

We come to this heawse an' this street when we wed,
An' t'childer wor born here, Eawr Frank an Eawr Ted,
An' we hoped we'd be buried fro' here--but instead
    We're beawn to be flittin' i' t'mornin'.

They offered us t'chance of an Old People's Flat
Wheer yo walk miles to t'shops an' yo corn'd keep a cat,
But we said to each other: It's noan come to *that*
    Wherever we flit to i' t'mornin'!"

Eawr Frank didn't want us, he's under her thumb,
(Hoo's posh, hoo'd fur shame fer his owd Dad an' Mum)
But Ted, bless him, sent us a wire 'at said "Come!"
    An' we're oaf to Australia i' t' mornin'!

Th'owd street's sin some patches o' good an' bad luck,
But we're danged if we're stoppin' to see wersels stuck,
An' aw t'grand years together just trodden i' t'muck
    When t'Motorway comes some fine mornin'.

So goodbye to Lancs. an' to owd friends an' true,
It's a heck of a change an' a lung way to goo,
But yo're never too owd to do wod yo mun doo---
    An' *that's* why we're flittin' i' t'mornin'!

A QUESTION OF MORALITY

G. C. Miller

"ANY play as deals wi' owd Nero an' ancient Rome," declared Councillor Dolittle, with the air of an oracle, "mun of necessity be both immoral an' indecent."

"Aw dunnot see for why, "grunted his worship the Mayor, doubtfully. "They had their good points, had th' Romans, tha knows."

"Such as---?" sneered the other.

"Well, they invented bread and circuses," insisted his worship. "There's nowt much ailin' fooak as con appreciate a good circus."

"It's their morals aw'm concerned about," said Dolittle grimly, "an' especially owd Nero's."

"Tell us more," said Councillor Wrynot. "Aw've heard as he war a bit of a hot 'un."

"Happen he'd a lot to put up wi'," suggested Councillor Greenwhistle sympathetically. "A naggin' wife or summat."

"He punched one of his wives to death," snapped Dolittle.

"There tha art," said Greenwhistle, shrugging his shoulders. "See what aw mean? Hoo mun ha' led him a dog's life."

The Watch Committee of Guildborough town council were reviewing an application from a touring company of players to stage a somewhat controversial play on the boards of the old Theatre Royal, and the puritan element on the council regarded such an innovation with grave misgivings. Hence the controversy.

"How about his mother then?" demanded Dolittle. "He drowned her, to say nowt about poisonin' his mother-in-law an' hauf a dozen members o' th'royal family."

"We all have our domestic problems," commented Alderman Noggin resignedly. "What else ha'n yo getten against him?'

"He fiddled while Rome war burnin'" suggested Councillor Noddy.

"What else could he do?" asked Doctor Grimes wearily, "He warn't a member o' th' fire brigade, war he?"

"Any reference to suchlike carryin's on" said Dolittle, "is bound to have a demoralisin' effect on th'community."

"Aw don't see why," said the medico. "th'owd lad's been

deead two thousand year. Connot yo let him rest in his grave?"

"That's what aw'm tryin' to do," retorted Dolittle, "It's these play-actors as are diggin' him up."

"Well, if we're bound to ban this domestic comedy o' theirs," said the chairman, "We's ha' to have summat specific. There's no point in revivin' all these Roman scandals 'bout pinnin' some of 'em down. We know he had five hundred wives, but all these emperors were summon extravagant in that line."

"Yo'n getten him mixed up wi' King Solomon," protested Noddy. "Aw once read as he had a wife for every day in th'year, an' they war that jealous he had to kiss 'em all round every mornin' afore breakfast."

"He wouldn't want any breakfast after samplin' all that lot," chuckled Wrynot, "especially if he war allergic to lip-stick!"

"It all boils down to a question o' morality," said Noddy, "whether tha believes in polygamy or monotony."

"What's th' difference?" asked Greenwhistle suspiciously.

"If tha keeps a harem full o' wild women, it's polygamy; if tha's nobbut one, it's monotony."

"Unless hoo's a film star," qualified Wrynot. "Aw could name one or two o' that lot as would ha' found owd Solomon hissel a full-time job."

"Aw dunnot suppose they're any worse nor other women," said Greenwhistle. "It's a case o' adverse publicity. Once th'art famous, tha has thi private life under th' microscope o' public opinion, an' after that tha con do nowt right. If tha nobbut goes for a six month cruise in a millionaire's private yacht, somebody'll tak' it th'wrong road."

"Especially thi husband," suggested Noggin, "if he happens to be a bit straight-laced."

"T'glare o' publicity," said Noddy, "has a tendency to mak' a woman eccentric an' flout convention. The wine of adulation goes to her heead, as yo mut say."

"True enough," agreed Greenwhistle ruefully, "an' once hoo goes off t'rails, tha con do no more good wi' her. Like when aw bought my missus a gold snake bangle."

"Did it bite her, or summat?" asked Wrynot, incredulously.

"It war me as war bitten," sighed Greenwhistle. "Hoo said hoo

hadn't a rag in her wardrobe hoo could wear wi' it, an' aw'd to fit her up wi' a new rig-out fro' top to toe."

"A married man," interposed doctor Grimes, "ought to have a workin' knowledge o' female psychology afore he goes on his honeymoon."

"If he did that" retorted Greenwhistle bitterly, "he'd never have a honeymoon, because he'd never get wed."

"It tak's 'em different roads," said Noddy. "Some are amenable to reason. There war one owd dowager duchess as made a blue-blooded member o't' nobility wheel her round th'estate in a wheel-barrow because hoo said he war out o' condition an' needed th'exercise. But when he dropped down dead hoo war t'first to admit hoo'd made a mistake."

"Will somebody tell me," asked the chairman, breathing heavily, "what's th' connection between owd Nero an' a' dowager duchess in a wheel-barrow? Aw may be a bit slow on th'uptake but aw'm allus willin' to learn."

"Aw'm nubbut pointin' a moral," said Noddy.

"Then stick to th'point tha'rt pointin' at," snapped his worship, "an' leave th' aristocracy alone. They'n enough to put up wi', what wi' income tax an' death duties."

"We connot ignore th'plain facts of history," said the medico. "If owd Nero war a wrong 'un (an' aw wouldn't ha' liked him for a Sunday School teacher misel) what about Henry VIII?"

"What about him?" demanded Greenwhistle heatedly.

"Nowt, only he used to knock his women-folk about a bit," said the doctor, "an' we con read about him in all th'history books."

"He war a victim o' connubiality," said Noddy.

"He warn't a good mixer, that was his trouble," suggested Greenwhistle. "He didn't like his wives gaddin' off to dances an' sich like, leavin' him ceawrd at whooam in th'chimney corner, so he put his foot down."

"An' chopped their heads off," said the chairman. "But what does that prove?"

"He war tryin' to work out a moral principle," said Noddy, "as never got beyond th'experimental stage."

"What principle?" demanded the other, inexorably

"Aw connot rightly say," confessed Noddy, "but he mun ha' had summat at th' back of his mind."

"Ay, plain murder," growled Noggin, "He even wrote a song about it, when he spiflicated poor Anne Boleyn."

"Aw never heard about it," said doctor Grimes, incredulously. "Does tha mean 'Greensleeves'?"

"Could be," agreed the alderman. "The chorus begins: 'Wi her head tucked underneath her arm.' "

"Well, he warn't exactly an advocate o' women's rights, aw must admit," conceded Greenwhistle. "But aw still think he's been misunderstood."

"They tell me her ghost still haunts th'Bloody Tower," said Noddy.

"Hoo'll soon ha' thine for company, if tha doesn't stick to th'point," said the chairman morosely. "An' aw hope tha finds that dowager duchess waitin' for thi wi' her wheel-barrow."

"This discussion doesn't seem to be gettin' us anywhere," said Doctor Grimes, glumly, "an' we'n covered a deal o'ground, rangin' fro' naggin' wives an' poisoned mother-in-laws to Henry V111 an' moral principles. Aw move as we just let nature take its own course an' let yon play-actors go right ahead. It'll teach us one thing anyroad."

"An' what might that be?" asked Dolittle.

"We's find out how many wives owd Nero really had," retorted the medico, "an' that should settle one argument, even if it contraves a corporation byelaw!"

TRAILES FUNERAL PARLOUR HAD CHARGE OF THE ARRANGEMENTS

Irvine Hunt

Dear friends I must apologise for cancelling my
funeral
but the patient, against all odds,
recovered.
The doctor's diagnosis proved suspiciously
incorrect
and now we've eaten the ham, against all odds,
ourselves
for breakfast lunch tea supper
breakfast
lunch tea supper again for
you know,
must know, how it is with ham.

Sir, it's not our wish to be unjust or
pressing
but three times now our bills have been
ignored.
Were workmanship in question we could
understand
the hitch. However do be
assured
it is not our wish to be unjust or
pressing:
just please return our coffin.

Most of the wreaths went back to the
senders
just as soon as we knew because it would have been
wasteful
to have kept so many flowers for home
décor.
But those retained were hung on
pictures,
doors over beds the fridge the oven and
the loo
and, nicely watered, they brighten our long
winter
especially the messages, especially.

Eight-six suddenly bought black
ties
seventy-four re-pressed black
dresses
nineteen yards of flyproof
veil
thirty-two will-make-do pairs of
shoes
and one-hundred-and-sixty
handkerchieves
for sniffs snorts flies in eyes
dust on cuffs
and indiscreet seagulls unable to
appreciate
the beauty of car windscreens.

So under the bed instead of a
jerry
is a blanket box with silver
handles
and the air is rank with lilies
roses
silver-papered fern. I don't like
cancelling
parties at the best of
times.
I think I'll change our doctor.

BLACK MAGIC

Gwen Horsfield

THE presence of a stranger in the 'The Eagle's Head' was not an event likely to cause a stir. But there was something about the old man which set him apart from the rest of the customers and caused us regulars to glance continually in his direction, and speculate silently as to who he was and where he had come from. He had a shabby-genteel sort of look, and you knew that if he spoke it would reveal a different accent from the broad, flat tones usually heard in these parts.

Tonight business was quiet, but not unusually so for a bitterly cold Monday, with the clock barely showing eight-thirty. As yet, of our regular crowd, there were only three—Bill Stewart, the book-maker; Dick Mercer, the accountant, and myself. And, expansive and generous, with a spicy wit and a broad welcome, the landlord, Tom Eddleston.

The conversation was a dull, flat affair, consisting of brief remarks interspersed by longish intervals of silence, during which we leant on the bar and watched Tom busy at his never-ending ritual of polishing. At last the door opened, letting in a chilly blast and Bob Withington, clutching the inevitable newspaper.

"How do, everybody?"

We returned his greeting.

"Not so warm tonight."

"You've said it."

"A pint o' mild, Tom"

Tom sprang to and delivered the beer. Bob opened his newspaper and disappeared behind it immediately. Another silence. The old man sat gazing into the fire, oblivious of everybody, his only movement to lift his glass occasionally. I watched him closely. That profile had never come from ordinary folk. They were the bones of breeding, the skin covering them dry and yellow, like parchment. His head drooped forward, and although his eyes were hidden you knew from his shoulders and the lines at his mouth and temples that he had suffered. His right hand held his glass; his left rested lightly on the shabby overcoat covering his knee. Dead, hopeless-looking hands they were.

Presently Bob spoke, and all but the old man looked up.

"Listen to this: 'Black Magic in Manchester. Woman accuses neighbour of putting curse on her. Claims compensation'. What d'you think of that?"

Tom laughed outright. "Not much. Some 'ope she's got. T'woman must be crackers."

"An eye to business, more likely," said Bill.

"What's the evil eye supposed to have done?" asked Dick.

"Oh, wished her bad luck and ill health," replied Bob. "Since then, she claims, she has lost all her money and had one operation after another."

"That'll be no 'ardship," grinned Tom. "Women love their operations."

"How does she go on with the compensation?" asked Dick.

"She doesn't get it, of course."

"Ah should think not!" exclaimed Tom in disgust. "A screw loose, is yon woman. What does she think this is? T'Middle Ages? Black Magic! Tuh!"

"Oh, I don't know," protested Bob. "In the Far East they firmly believe in it. I remember---"

" 'Ot climate," put in Tom like a shotgun. " 'Ypnotises 'em. 'Ot climate an' ignorance — perfect combination for that sort of rubbish."

"I was reading only the other day that they believe in it in Italy," I put in.

"Well, this is Lankisheer, not Italy nor t' Far East; an' that sort o' rot went out wi' owd Mother Demdyke."

"But lots of people believe in it now," said Dick.

"Would you like me to tell you a story, gentlemen? A true story."

This remark, delivered so quietly and unexpectedly, caused us to turn in astonishment. The old man had suddenly come to life and was looking at us with the strangest expression. We all stared at him, speechless, almost resenting the intrusion. But Tom, with his usual tact, saved the situation.

"A story, sir?" he said, smiling. "Certainly. Always ready for a good story in this pub."

"I do hope you will forgive me for butting in, but you were speaking of Black Magic. I think I have something which might interest you."

"Carry on, sir."

"Well, I shall have to take you to London thirty years ago. I was in the antique trade—a well-established family business of many generations. Our integrity was unquestionable; our contacts, business and social, the best. I married late, and it was not until ten years after the marriage that we were blessed with a son. We called him Charles.

Naturally we doted on the boy and wanted only the best for him—education, clothes, friends: in fact, everything to produce a perfect gentleman. And I might say we were not disappointed. He was a credit to us. Imagine, therefore, our delight when he expressed a wish to come into the business. He proved an apt pupil and soon proved to have a flair for the work—almost an instinct."

"Like me wi' t'beer," laughed Tom. "Sorry, sir, carry on!"

"Well, since we mixed with people of taste and refinement, we naturally expected our son to turn in that direction for a wife. But no, the girl Charles picked up had neither taste nor refinement. To think that Charles, whose taste had always been beyond question, should fail so lamentably in this, the most important thing of his life! We were astounded."

"I expect she was easy on the eye," said Bill.

"Yes—er—in a crude sort of way."

"Warm 'eart, I expect," put in Tom feelingly. "Appen 'e found t'girls 'e knew a bit on the 'aughty side."

"Perhaps," replied the old man. "However, such a match was out of the question and I determined to put a stop to it."

"A bit risky, that," said Tom. "I allus say, 'let 'em please theirsels'."

"What did you do?" asked Dick.

"My wife and I pleaded, almost went on our knees, but it was useless. Then I appealed to the girl and that failed."

"What did you do then?" I asked. "Give up?"

"Oh, no. By now the thing had become an obsession. My one thought, day and night, was to save my son. Then one day, going over my treasures in the shop, I came across a curio I had bought from an Egyptian some time previously. A little bronze idol. Intrinsically it was of little value, but the Egyptian claimed it had certain peculiarities. He said it must never be given—always sold. If given it would assume evil characteristics, and the recipient was likely to meet with violence or untimely death." He paused and took a drink, then went on

"I took this with a pinch of salt, of course, but with a certain customer in mind who I knew would be intrigued with such a novelty, I bought it. I then forgot all about it. But as I picked it up that day I could hear the Egyptian's words. Nonsense, I told myself. But already a plan was forming in my mind."

"Of course it were nonsense," said Tom.

"Quite. Nevertheless, I knew what I was going to do. I would give this charm---this 'lucky' charm---to my daughter-in-law as a small wedding gift."

"Phew!" said Dick. "You must have been desperate."

"I was," replied the old man. "Not only desperate: obsessed! I read all I could on Black Magic and would sit for hours before the little idol, willing my evil desires to take effect."

I felt my spine beginning to creep. Everybody had stopped drinking.

"Did you stop the wedding?" I asked.

"No, they got married." He paused. "The car overturned on their honeymoon."

"And was the girl killed?" asked Dick.

"No. . . My son was killed."

We all gasped.

" 'Ard luck, sir," said Tom, quickly.

"When they brought him home we found this in his pocket." He brought out a small bronze object which he handed to me.

"Not the---?" I asked.

"The very same. She had given it to him, hoping to pass on the luck I had told her it would bring."

I shivered, and passed the little idol round.

"My wife died soon after, from shock."

"That was bad," sympathised Tom. "Terrible."

"And what happened to the girl?" asked Bill.

"She went away. I never saw her again."

"But aren't you afraid to carry this about with you? I mean, after all that---?"

"Not at all. Remember, the thing had to be bought. Well, I had paid for it First my son, then my wife and finally my business, which I fear I let go to pieces. What had I left?"

He gazed tragically in front of him.

"Look closely on the bottom," he said. "You will find some markings."

I did so.

"What would you imagine they were?" "Well, I'm not an expert," I said, "but I suppose they could be Egyptian hieroglyphics."

"So I thought until I examined them through this." He took out a small magnifying glass which he handed to me. I peered through it. The words were quite clear. I read them aloud. *MADE IN BIRMINGHAM.*

THREE OWD MAIDS

Harvey Kershaw

Mi onsetters were born an' bred
I' what were t'country once, it's said,
They thrived on t'moorlond breeze;
Anent tu t'cot, hutched up together,
Keepin' a watch on time an' weather,
There stood three bonny trees.

Aw weel bethink, mi dear owd dad
Oft said: "Look at yon trees, mi lad,
They favvor three owd maids."
When t'strong wynts blew, then sure enough
Their moans were yerd reet deawn i' t'clough,
As th' owl-leet cast its shades.

When Aw first toddled off tu t'skoo',
As though they knew, they watched me goo,
An' waved their arms tu mi:
Then coomin' wom, o'er t'neighbourin' farms,
They welcomed mi wi' oppen arms,
Back into t'family.

I' winter time, like boggarts fow,
They'd scraggy arms an' white-capped brow,
As t'snow coom wi' a wuther;
But Springtime clothed their naked limbs,
Then they'd nod their yeds tu t'soft wynt's whims,
An' gossip, one tu t'other.

When Summer sun shone breet aboon,
Their branches hummed wi' merry tune,
As brids skimmed to an' fro;
Chill Autumn browt its russet leaf,
Then, as a woman scrikes i' grief,
Like tears, breawn leaves'd fo'.

But time an' change move quickly on,
Eawr folk, an' th'heawse Aw knew, are gone,
Yet nowt, their mem'ry fades;
Neaw blocks o' flats are built reawnd t'nook,
But th'trees were spared, an' if yo'll look,
Yo' con still see t'three owd maids.

THILERMAN

Miranda Roberts

S HOULD you ask someone where they are thinking of going for their holidays this year and they answer 'Thilerman', don't imagine they mean the Yangtse River, the Dutch East Indies, or even Holland. They mean that bit of land reputed to have been flung in anger from the hand of a giant of long ago---in other words, the Isle of Man.

The first time I went there I was aged two-years-three-and-a-half-months, and I remember quite clearly seeing some Polar bears in a pool with a rail round, and also—I can remember huge green waves shooting up on either side of the ship!

It was a long time after that when I went to Thilerman again. I was supposed to be a responsible adult, yet on my head was a coolie-type straw hat! A large flat hat, a rather expensive hat, and the reason I wore it on my head was simply that I had nowhere else to put it. It wouldn't go in my bag, which already bulged, and I couldn't carry an out-sized paper hat-bag in addition to all the other clobber with which I was burdened---so I just stuck it on my head.

It was a pity that as soon as I got on board the ship a strong wind got up, and I had to hold onto the thing with one hand whilst trying to get down into the saloon with my luggage.

"Tek your luggage down with you!" I had been advised. "Yon fellers chucks it all o'er t'place, an' all t'corners comes off!"

Well, I got down, hat and all, and the ship got well away. I soon felt so horrible below decks that I decided to go up again, so back I went, clutching bags and hat, to find a real Nor' Nor.easter belting us about like a match-box. How I wished I had on a Sou' Souwester! For in addition to a hundred-mile-an-hour gale it had started raining heavily. There seemed to be nobody but me on that side of the ship, except some tough-looking bods battening down the hatches.

"Everybody on t'other side!" bellowed one hoarsely, so I sped round as directed, to find the ship listing badly, doubtless from the press of people. Everybody seemed to be rapidly turning green, so back I went to the side I had come from, which was now high up out of the water. I didn't know whether it was the starboard or port side---and I didn't care.

I had taken a lot of advice about seasickness remedies and as I now felt very seasick I got the half-lemon out of my pocket and began to suck it. As it emptied, great fans of spray kept bounding over the ship's side, filling it up like a wine-glass, as well as drenching me through! My coolie-hat was now over my nose, and a sharp point stuck up on my crown. Feeling like death warmed-up I once again hurried round to the other side, dragging my bag, which I put down in a dark corner and sat on. Immediately, somebody's upper dental-plate fell in my lap! That was it! That was all I needed.

Some kind soul (you've met 'em, they are *never* sick, and they eat meat pies all the way to 'Thilerman) some kind soul took my arm and piloted me below. I was just conscious enough to say loudly: "I wish the damn ship would go to the bottom!"

"Don't talk so daft," she said pleasantly. "You've got to come back yet!"

I stayed in the 'little room' until a stewardess hooked me out, put me to bed in the ladies' lounge with a rug, and brought me a cup of tea. There my friends found me---I had been lost ever since we got on board. They, too, looked as though they had been eating meat pies. I looked up as well as I was able to, and the so-called friends at once burst into shrieks of wild hysterical laughter.

"Oh, dear! You've still got your hat on! You look exactly like one of those beautiful goffered lampshades!"

"I *feel* like a beautiful goffered lampshade, too," I croaked.

Somehow in that high tide the boat landed, after knocking a few planks off its side, but I didn't begin to enjoy my holiday until the Wednesday. Every time I put a foot down, the pavements seemed to heave up into my face. Besides, I had nightmares every night when I remembered the words: "You've got to come back yet!"

The weather was lovely all week until the Friday night before our return, when another gale blew up. With the despairing calm of the condemned, I gave in.

"If I've to die," I thought, "I'll die,"--- and spent all my remaining money on boxes of kippers which I sent to friends safe at home. "At least they'll remember me kindly when I'm gone!" I thought sadly.

Yes, it *was* terrible going back---just as rough as it had been coming. I took the precaution of using one of my secret remedies---a sheer bit of witchcraft, this:-

"Fasten a band of brown paper about nine inches wide all round the body, on the bare skin from the waist down."

My friends had another good laugh at my expense when I told them, and kept poking at me to hear me crackle. I had the supreme satisfaction of leading them, one by one, half-dead, below---whilst I, *I ate meat pies all the way home!*

WELCOME, BONNY BRID

Samuel Laycock (1826-1893)

Tha'rt welcome, little bonny brid,
But shouldn't ha' come just when tha did;
Toimes are bed.
We're short o' pobbies for eawr Joe,
But that, of course, tha didn't know,
Did ta, lad?

Aw've often yeard mi feyther tell,
'At when aw coom i' th'world misel'
Trade wur slack;
And neaw it's hard wark pooin' throo---
But aw munno fear thee,---iv aw do
Tha'll go back.

Cheer up! these toimes'll awter soon;
Aw'm beawn to beigh another spoon---
One for thee:---
An' as tha's sich a pratty face
Aw'll let thi have eawr Charley's place
On mi knee.

God bless thi, love! aw'm fain tha'rt come,
Just try and mak' thisel awhoam:
Here's thi nest;
Tha'rt loike thi mother to a tee,
But tha's thi feyther's nose, aw see,
Well, aw'm blest!

Come, come, tha needn't look so shy,
Aw am no' blamin' thee, not I;
Settle deawn,
An' tak' this haupney for thisel',
Ther's lots of sugar-sticks to sell
Deawn i' th'teawn.

Aw know when first aw coom to th'leet,
Aw're fond o' owt 'at tasted sweet;
Tha'll be t'same.
But come, tha's never towd thi dad
What he's to co thi yet, mi lad,
What's thi name?

Hush! Hush! tha mustn't cry this way,
But get this sope o' cinder tay
While it's warm;
Mi mother used to give it me,
When aw wur sich a lad as thee,
In her arm.

Hush-a-babby, hush-a-bee,---
Oh, what a temper!---dear-a-me
Heaw tha skrikes!
Here's a bit o' sugar, sithee;
Howd thi noise, an' then aw'll gie thee
Owt tha likes.

We've nobbut getten coarsish fare,
But, eawt o this tha'll get thi share,
Never fear.
Aw hope tha'll never want a meal,
But allus fill thi bally weel
While tha'rt here.

Thi feyther's noan been wed so lung,
An' yet tha sees he's middlin' thrung
Wi' yo' o.
Besides thi little brother Ted,
We've one upsteers, asleep i' bed,
Wi' eawr Joe.

But tho' we've childer two or three,
We'll mak' a bit o' reawm for thee,
Bless thee, lad!
Th'art th'prattiest brid we have i' th'nest,
So hutch up closer to mi breast,
Aw'm thi dad.

THE MARKET

Joan Pomfret

WHEN September came, putting an end to the brief northern summer and scattering the remaining tourists like a flock of migrant birds, Elizabeth remembered the market.. . .

They had warned her at home about marrying a foreigner and going to live in another country – said that she was too young to know her own mind and would have done better with Albert Norcross next door – but she had laughed at them. After all, as she kept telling them, Norway wasn't so very foreign, and *she* didn't want to stay all her life in a mill town under the moors and push babies up and down the steep streets she herself had played in. And Inge had seemed so different, so romantic – coming down the church on his arm in her white wedding dress and pearl coronet, she had felt like a queen, a Snow Queen out of a fairy tale, knowing that all the girls were envying her his fair proud looks and broad shoulders.

She and her mother had bought the material for her wedding dress on the market one Wednesday afternoon. It was a wonderful out-door market, said by many to be the best in the north of England, and ever since Elizabeth was a little girl they had done most of their shopping there. Now, when she closed her eyes, she could see the stalls set out on the big cobbled square near the town hall – the fruits and vegetables spilling their bright colours like a French painting – the flower stalls – the cheeses – and, best of all, the materials. If you threaded your way down the middle of the stalls they caught your eye at every turn as they blew in the draughts or lay in vivid heaps under the awnings. Silks, satins, cottons, nylons, lengths of tweed – a good needlewoman (and most Lancashire women *were* good needlewomen) – could find anything she wanted there, from new lace curtains to children's pyjamas or an evening gown. Once, Elizabeth remembered, her mother had bought a remnant of clover-coloured wool and made her a little fur-trimmed coat; later on in her 'teens she had made her first dance dress.; there had been blouses, too, and skirts, and a dressing-gown embroidered with scarlet birds – all her life, it seemed, had been closely wrapped up with the market on Wednesday afternoons!

That had been one of the first things she missed when the homesickness started, and Inge became a gloomy, silent stranger; that, and all the other familiar sights of her home-town. The public library, with its thousands of books, the cinemas, the park, the Mecca ballroom where she and her friends had danced on Saturday nights. She thought with longing of toasted tea-cakes in the market café, and of the worn green-upholstered chairs where she and her parents had watched television by a blazing coal fire. She remembered the Grammer School caps and the colour of the local buses; she even remembered Albert Norcross, stolid and dependable, cutting the hedge in the garden next door — "It was a nice little town," she thought with a pang, forgetting how it had bored her a year ago. "I shall never know any place quite so well again!" And then she would think of those wastes of sea which separated her from it, and when she imagined the coming winter she was filled with dread.

She knew by now what to expect, for it was September, and in another few weeks the first snow would fall. It would pile up against the doorway of Inge's blue frame-house and block the dirt roads. The sledges or 'sparks' would be brought out, and the sun would sink lower and lower in the sky until one day in November it would not rise at all. 'Our bright days are done and we are for the dark' — who was it said that, and where had she heard it? Elizabeth did not know, but she said it over and over again until one day she could bear it no longer.

"I want to go home," she said to Inge, "oh, how I want to go home!"

"Perhaps next year," he said, unperturbed.

"No, now. This instant. I *must* go home before the Darkness."

"It is not possible." Inge stared at her with that cold proud look. "You are being silly. We have not the money for you to go to England."

"My dad will send it," she told him defiantly.

"No, you cannot go."

"I will, I will!" she shouted at him. "I can't stand it any longer! I never thought it would be like this — the rain, the cold, no-one to talk to, and the dark days coming. They say it'll be dark all the time. I can't spend the rest of my life here. I'd rather die!"

"Then of course you must go," Inge said wearily at last. "I did not know you felt this way."

She had expected one of their furious quarrels, not this cold, deadly indifference. Her voice softened a little.

"Perhaps — after a while — I should feel more able to face it. To come back —"

"No," Inge said. "No. If you go now you will never come back. . ."

If he had kissed her then, or talked to her, things might have been different, but after that day he scarcely spoke again. Even on the last evening when he carried her cases to the south-bound coastal-ship he made no attempt to persuade her to change her mind. He just said: "Farvel, Elizabeth," and they shook hands like strangers. She saw him standing proud and aloof under the lamps on the quay, then, as the ship swung round into a rough sea and a curtain of rain, he was gone.

On the first Wednesday afternoon afterwards, Elizabeth and her mother went to the market. It was just the same, or at least it seemed so at first, and they walked slowly, arm in arm, up and down the stalls as they had always done. There were the fruits and vegetables glowing through the frosty grey of the October afternoon — the shrimps, the cheeses, the gay plastic buckets and the hands of the Market Hall clock pointing to half-past three. They bought a length of blue tweed to make Elizabeth a winter frock, and a linen tea towel with pictures of English inns on it. They stopped and chattered with friends — excited friends, discreetly sympathetic friends, blatantly curious friends — who asked straight out if Elizabeth had left her husband and why she had come home.

"Yes, it was a mistake," she heard her mother whisper. "It didn't work out. Well, *I* didn't want her to go up there in the first place! Just imagine — our Elizabeth stuck up there in an Arctic fishing port! Yes. . .yes. . .terribly lonely. . .and all that smelly fish! A dreadful place. . ."

Elizabeth looked away, her eyes pricking with tears. No, she wanted to say to them, no, it wasn't a dreadful place at all. When the ice melted on the lakes and summer came, it was beautiful. The sea was the colour of jade between the islands, and all the little birch trees feathery-green — was it her imagination, or did everything here at home look dirty and drab? There was a thick coat of soot on the Victorian town hall, and the gutters were slimy with chip-papers and orange peel. The Lancashire speech she heard on every side sounded crude and rough, and the market men's cloth caps and red hands looked revolting.

She turned away and found that she was looking at the stall where they had bought the white brocade for her wedding dress. There was another roll there now, waiting for some luckier bride, and close to it, draped over a rail, a cascading length of blue velvet the colour of a northern sky, the colour of Inge's little house. . .

"Come along love," she heard her mother call. "Quarter to four — time for our teas!" and she followed her through the market, suddenly heartsick for those blue walls, the tonk-tonk of the fishing boats, and that white church against its crazy back-cloth of mountain. But then, *women* — as Inge Johansen was saying a thousand miles away at that very moment — "Vimmen always wish to be in some place they are not. I do not understand vimmen at all!"

OWD PENDLE

R. Y. Digby

Aw've ollus lov'd owd Pendle Hill,
Aw someheaw think Aw ollus will;
Durnt co' mi daft iv neaw Aw tell
Heaw Pendle casts o' me a spell.

Id must ha' bin a flaysome seet
When Pendle's beacon blazed i' t'neet,
An' t'wizard Demdyke, mockin', stood,
While deawn th'hill-side ther' poured thick mud.

Aw'm glad i' t'countryside areawnd
Ther's no mooar wizards to bi feawnd,
Nor witches---bud ther's magic still
Up o' yon wild an' looanly hill.

Ther's magic i' th'owd curlew's cry,
I' t'moanin' wind an' th'angry sky;
An' i'breet dew-drops—glist'nin pearls—
As t'mornin' mist i' t'sun unfurls.

Fro' t'Coppice, t'other side o' t'Dale,
Aw'm ollus fain yon hill to hail,
Id welly seeams to toak to me,
Aw'll luv yon hill till t'day Aw dee.

THE BAR GAIST

John Roby (1793–1850)

NOT far from the little snug smoky village of Blakeley, or Blackley, there lies one of the most romantic dells, rejoicing in a state of singular seclusion, and in the oldest of Lancashire names, to wit, the "Boggart-hole". Rich in every requisite for picturesque beauty and poetical association, it is impossible for me (who am neither a painter nor a poet) to describe this dell as it should be described; and I will therefore only beg of thee, gentle reader, who peradventure mayst not have lingered in this classical neighbourhood, to fancy a deep, deep dell, its steep sides fringed down with hazel and beech, and fern and thick undergrowth, and clothed at the bottom with the richest and greenest sward in the world. You descend, clinging to the trees, and scrambling as best you may---and now you stand on haunted ground! Tread softly, for this is the Boggart's clough; and see in yonder dark corner, and beneath the projecting mossy stone, where that dusky sullen cave yawns before us, like a bit of Salvator's best, there lurks the strange elf, the sly and mischievous Boggart. Bounce! I see him coming; oh no, it was only a hare bouncing from her form; there it goes---there!

I will tell you of some of the pranks of this very Boggart, and how he teased and tormented a good farmer's family in a house hard by, and I assure you it was a very worthy old lady who told me the story. But first, suppose we leave the Boggart's demesne and pay a visit to the theatre of his strange doings.

You see that old farmhouse about two fields distant, shaded by the sycamore-tree: that was the spot which the Boggart or Bar-gaist selected for his freaks; there he held his revels, perplexing honest George Cheetham---for that was the farmer's name---scaring his maids, worrying his men, and frightening the poor children out of their seven senses, so that at last not even a mouse durst show himself indoors at the farm, as he valued his whiskers, five minutes after the clock had struck twelve.

It had long been remarked that whenever a merry tale was told on a winter's evening a small shrill voice was heard above all the rest, like a baby's penny trumpet, joining in with the laughter.

"Weel laughed, Boggart, thou'rt a fine little tyke, I's warrant, if one could but just catch glent on thee," said Robert, the youngest of the farmer's sons, early one evening, a little before Christmas, for familiarity had made them somewhat bold with their invisible guest. Now, though more pleasant stories were told on that night beside the hearth than had been told there for the three preceding months, though the fire flickered brightly, though all the faces around it were full of mirth and happiness, and though everything, it might seem, was there which could make even a Boggart enjoy himself, yet the small shrill laugh was heard no more that night after little Bob's remark.

Robert, who was a short, stout fellow for his age, slept in the same bed as his elder brother John, who was reckoned an uncommonly fine and tall lad for his years. No sooner had they got fairly sleep than they were roused by the small shrill voice in their room shouting out, "Little tyke, indeed! little tyke thysel! Ho, ho, ho! I'll have my laugh now---Ho, ho, ho!"

The room was completely dark, and all in and about the house was so still that the sound scared them fearfully. The concluding screech made the place echo again;--- but this strange laughter was not necessary to prevent little Robert from further sleep, as he found himself one moment seized by the feet and pulled to the bottom of the bed, and the next moment dragged up again on his pillow. This was no sooner done than by the same invisible power, he was pulled down again, and then his head would be dragged back, and placed as high as his brother's.

"Short and long won't match,---short and long won't match,---ho, ho, ho!" shouted the well-known voice of the Boggart, between each adjustment of little Robert with his tall brother, and thus were they both wearied for more than a hundred times; yet so great was their terror, that neither Robert nor his brother--- "Long John" as he ever afterwards was called---dared to stir one inch; and you may well suppose how delighted they both were when the first grey light of morning appeared.

"We'st now ha' some rest, happen" said John, turning on his side in the expectation of a good nap, and covering himself with the bedclothes, which the pulling of Robert so often backwards and forwards had tumbled about sadly.

"Rest!" said the same voice that had plagued them throughout the night, "rest---what is rest? Boggart knows no rest."

"Plague tak' thee for a Boggart!" said the farmer next morning, on hearing the strange story from his children: "Plague tak' thee! can thee not let the poor things be quiet? But I'll be up with thee, my gentleman: so tak' th'chamber an' be hanged to thee, if thou wilt. Jack and Little Robert shall sleep o'er the cart-house, and Boggart may rest or wriggle as he likes when he is by himself!"

The move was accordingly made, and the bed of the brothers transferred to their new sleeping-room over the cart-house, where they remained for some time undisturbed; but his Boggartship having now fairly become the possessor of a room at the farm, it would appear, considered himself in the light of a privileged inmate, and not, as hitherto, an occasional visitor, who merely joined in the general expression of merriment. Familiarity, they say, breeds contempt; and now the children's bread and butter would be snatched away, or their porringers of bread and milk would be dashed to the ground by an unseen hand; or if the younger ones were left alone but for a few minutes, they were sure to be found screaming with terror on the return of their nurse. Sometimes, however, he would behave himself kindly. The cream was then churned, and the pans and kettles scoured without hands. There was one circumstance which was remarkable;—the stairs ascended from the kitchen, a partition of boards covered the ends of the steps, and formed a closet beneath the staircase. From one of the boards of this partition a large round knot was accidentally displaced; and one day the youngest of the children, while playing with the shoe-horn, stuck it into this knot-hole. Whether or not the aperture had been formed by the Boggart as a peep-hole to watch the motions of the family, I cannot pretend to say. Some thought it was, for it was called the Boggart's peep-hole; but others said that they had remembered it long before the shrill laugh of the Boggart was heard in the house. However this may have been, it is certain that the horn was ejected with surprising precision at the head of whoever put it there; and either in mirth or anger the horn was darted forth with great velocity, and stuck the poor child over the ear.

There are few matters upon which parents feel more acutely than that of the maltreatment of their offspring; but time, that great soother of all things, at length familiarised this dangerous occurrence to everyone at the farm, and that which at the first was regarded with the utmost terror, became a kind of amusement with the more thoughtless and daring of the family.

Often was the horn slipped slyly into the hole, and in return it never failed to be flung at the head of some one, but most commonly at the person who placed it there. They were used to call this pastime, in the provincial dialect, "laking wi' t'Boggart"; that is, playing with the Boggart. An old tailor, whom I but faintly remember, used to say that the horn was often "pitched" at his head, and at the head of his apprentice, whilst seated here on the kitchen table, when they went their rounds to work, as is customary with country tailors. At length the goblin, not contented with flinging the horn, returned to his night persecutions. Heavy steps, as of a person in wooden clogs, were at first heard clattering downstairs in the dead hour of darkness; then the pewter and earthen dishes appeared to be dashed on the kitchen-floor; though in the morning all remained uninjured on their respective shelves. The children generally were marked out as objects of dislike by their unearthly tormentor. The curtains of their beds would be violently pulled to and fro,---then a heavy weight, as of a human being, would press them nearly to suffocation, from which it was impossible to escape. The night, instead of being the time for repose, was disturbed with screams and dreadful noises, and thus was the whole house alarmed night after night. Things could not long continue in this fashion; the farmer and his good dame resolved to leave a place where they could no longer expect rest or comfort; and George Cheetham was actually following with his wife and family the last load of furniture, when they were met by a neighbouring farmer, named John Marshall.

"Well, Georgey, and soa you're leaving th'owd house at last?" said Marshall.

"Heigh, Johnny, ma lad, I'm in a manner forced to't, thou sees," replied the other; "for that wearyfu' Boggart torments us soa, we can neither rest neet nor day for't. It seems loike to have a malice agin't young uns,---an' it ommost kills my poor dame here at thoughts on't, and soa thou sees we're forc'd to flit like."

He had got thus far in his complaint, when, behold, a shrill voice from a deep upright churn, the topmost utensil on the cart, called out---"Ay, ay, neighbour, we're flitting, you see."

" 'Od rot thee!" exclaimed George, "if I'd known thou'd been flitting too, I wadn't ha stirred a peg. Nay, nay,---it's no use, Mally," he continued, turning to his wife, "we may as weel turn back again to th'owd house as be tormented in another not so convenient."

They did return; but the Boggart, having from the occurrence ascertained the insecurity of his tenure, became less outrageous, and was never more guilty of disturbing, in any extraordinary degree, the quiet of the family.

BROSSEN QUARRY

Irvine Hunt

Twice Brossen's thunder startles
the Furness fells.
Even in snow the quarry men
nag the mountain with
dynamite and drill.
Slate, sharp hewn, tumbles
at their touch.
Suddenly exposed, stone
spews the quarry floor,
and where that appears
is more.

This is no sudden thing:
centuries gone men hewed
with sharpened metal,
the dull ring of iron
striking sparks,
digging the cumbersome
with the smooth.

It looks tough too tough
to shape but rock,
stubborn enough to chisel
and hammer, melts at the
diamond saw.

The explosive whirl
of ice and rock
scatters the sheep;
each year's flock learns
the lesson anew.
Only the crows,
hooked on the wind,
seem unhurried,
trading the pickings
of a carcass
for a view, safer
and loftier.

In Rusland's quiet woods
no one might tell
but for that muffled boom
that men still plundered
the stark flank of the fell.
Sunlit becks churn,
trees stir and relapse in
winter silence. The bang
dies and the woodland calm
is restored.

Intent, the quarry men
hammer away the day,
snatching cold stone from
the mountain, wrenching a
little loose before the trek
down-track to Coniston.
Soon the crows return to a
broken feast; there is a pause:
a pheasant scorches the fell
with abuse.

It seems a fair judgment.

TH'LAST BRICK

Harvey Fitton

IT wern't Jack Russell's fault 'at he wer' out o' wark; what wi' t'decline o' cotton an' th'owd Brock Mill givin' up th'ghost, it wer' a period o' unemployment o' round. Yo' 'ad either t'lev t'village er put up wi' what yo could get i' t'wark line.

Jack wer' one o' a group o' villagers 'at 'ad turn't up t'see th'end of' th'owd Brock chimney; t'demolition contractors 'ad warked fer two days gettin' it ready, an' today wer' t'day when th'chimney wer' t'com down.

"Dust know how lung yon chimney's bin stondin'?" he axed his mate Joe Gilks.

Joe's answer coom i' a flash. "Aye," he said, "thi started buildin' t'factory i' 1887, t'chimney wer' finished May 14th 1889."

"Tha surprises mi," replied Jack. "Ah knew it wer' 1889 when it wer' finished, but aw couldn't ha' getten down to th' exact date---how does tha know?"

"Becose it wer' mi gronfayther 'at built it," answered Joe.

"Thi gronfayther built it?" said Jack in surprise. "Aw allus thowt it wer' built wi' a firm co'ed Saxon's."

"Saxon's wer' th'contractors," replied Joe, "but mi gronfayther wer' t'Master Builder."

"Gilks---Gilks, by-go it rings a bell," said Jack. "Mi gronmother allus said Mr. Gilks."

"What th'heck 'as thi gronmother getten to do wi' it?" axed Joe.

"It's my turn t' gi' thee a surprise," said Jack. "Mi gronmother claimed t' ha' th'honour o' layin' th' last brick on that chimney---her fayther, mi great-gronfayther, wer' t' Managin' Director when t'Brock started up."

"Thi gronmother laid t' last brick on this chimney---how did hoo manage that?" axed Joe.

Jack grinned. "It's a family tale," he said, "it's bin honded down as tha might say, mi gronmother's towd mi about it monny a time."

"Thi gronmother 'ull be deaod now, aw reckon?" axed Joe.

"Aye," agreed Jack, "hoo'd ha' bin about ninety if hoo'd ha' lived, hoo wer' nobbut about ten when it happened."

"Then it's time aw yerd it," said Joe, "aw reckon when tha's finished we's bi vernee related."

"Like aw just towd thi, it's a family tale," replied Jack, "but it's true enough. What t'chimney we' vernee finished mi great-gronfayther 'ad a special brick made wi' mi gronmother's initials cut on it—M.B. Thi took her up t' chimney in a special basket; t'builder—th'gronfayther 'at tha lays claim to—wer' waitin' fer her on t'top; an' theer, wi' a little silver trowel in her hond, hoo laid th'last brick; wi han' that little silver trowel in t'top cupboard t' this day. It gad her summat t'talk about fer t'rest o' her life."

"Aw see," nodded Joe, "aw reckon in about ten minutes that brick 'ull bi n'ar t'ground ner it's bin fer som' time."

"Aye, an' aw'm bown t'see if aw con find it," said Jack.

"Tha's a betther chance o' findin' it now ner' ever tha 'ad," agreed Joe.

"Wait a bit," said Jack, howdin' his hond up. "Tha hasno' yerd o' th'tale yet, we'r comin' t'spicy bit. Just afore mi gronmother went up t'chimney, her fayther put a gowden sovereign in her hond, an. towd her t' press it into t'mortar afore hoo laid t'brick!"

"What!" gasped Joe. "A gowden sovereign under a brick marked wi' th'initials M.B.—then—then, it could bi theer yet!"

"Well, aw dunno," laughed Jack, "it depends what soart o' a mon thi gronfayther wer'."

"Tha's getten mi gaspin' now," replied Joe, "aw don't follow thi."

"Well, aw'll put it to thi straight," said Jack, "when mi gronmother coom down hoo left thi gronfayther up—when he coom down, t'chimney wer' finished."

Joe grinned. "Tha'rt noan insinuatin' 'at mi gronfayther pinched that gowd sovereign, arto?"

"Aye, aw am," laughed Jack. "Put thisel in his shop—theer he wer', next door t' a gowden sovereign 'at wouldn't see t'leet o' day as long as t'chimney stood; i' hawve a jiffy he hould ha' 'ad it out, re-laid t'brick, an' nobody 'ud ha' bin th'wiser."

"Aye," mused Joe. "an' so he could. A gowden sovereign wer' a lot o' brass in thoose days."

"It's still a lot o'brass," said Jack regretfully. "Aw wonder?"

"Aw wonder?" mused Joe.

215

Even as thi wer' wonderin' th'owd chimney gat a last shiverin' groan, an' slutter't down in a flurry o' bricks an' mortar.

"We'd bether keep this to 'ussels," whispered Jack.

"We'll ha' a look round t'morn when t'coast is clear," answered Joe.

"Howd on," said Jack, "let's goo about this i' gradely fashion; wi connut goo snoopin' about, or t'demolishers 'ull want t' know what we'r after."

"Hasto'onny suggestions?" axed Joe.

"Aw think aw know how t'goo about it," replied Jack, "Com' wi' me."

Jack made his road to t'chief demolisher an' axed him if he could collect som' o' th'bricks 'at 'adn't bin damaged. He towd him he wer' a bit sentimental about th'owd chimney, an' he'd like t'build hissel a greenhouse out o' th'rubble.

"Tak as monny as yo' like," said t'demolisher. "It'll be less fer us t'shift."

T'follow in' day seed Jack an' Joe scrabblin' round t' pile o' rubble bowt onnybody axin' questions---thi 'ad a wheelbarrow, a big hommer an' a couple o' crow-bars. Thi wandered t'wheer t'top part o'th'chimney 'ad leet, an' started t'root about.

"Wer' t'brick reet at t'top?" axed Joe.

"It wer' on th'topmost layer o' th'outside rim" replied Jack.

"It shouldn't be hard to find," said Joe, "look out fer th'initials M.B."

Thi rooted about till thi fun a reet clump o' bricks stuck together, about t'size an' t'shape o' a bucket. "Gi that lot a bang wi' thi hommer," said Jack, "an' then wi con turn it o'er."

Bang went Joe's hommer---an', they both seed it together---four bricks still howdin' together, but on t'topmost brick through t'muck an' dirt, thi could just mak' out M.B. Thi both stopped workin'. "So thi family tale wer' reet," said Joe. Jack put his hond on Joe's shoulder---"This is it, owd lad, it's muck or mawfin now---we's soon know what soart of a chap thi gronfayther wer'."

Joe gad th'bricks a gentle tap. "Wi munnat spyle th' special brick, tha'll want that as a souvenir, aw reckon."

"T'sovereign 'ud do mi more good," said Jack.

Two more taps, an' t'bricks parted company---thi both gazed excitedly at a gowden sovereign 'at wer' cased i' mortar but wer' still breet enough t'wink at 'em.

216

"Well," said Joe, "aw reckon this proves summat."

"Aw'll tell thi what it proves," answered Jack, scrattin' his yed, "it proves 'at thi gronfayther wer' an honest man, but a bit o' a foo' t'hissel."

"A bit o' a foo' t'hissel!" echoed Joe, "how dus't mak' that out?"

"Look round," said Jack, "what dusti see?---a pile o' bricks an' rubble, if aw hadno' known about it, what would ha' happened to t'sovereign?"

"Ther's no tellin'," agreed Joe, "what's bown t'happen to it now?"

"Aw reckon finders are keepers i' this case," said Jack. "We'll goo hawve an' hawve---one hawve aw inherit fro' mi gronmother, an' th'other hawve tha inherits fro' thi gronfayther---that road our conscience is clear."

"Aw couldn't agree wi' thi more," nodded Joe.

CLEYNIN' NEET

N. Pickles

On Thursda neets just after t'tay
Ah'd allus hear mi mother say
"Cum on lass, get t'blackleead brush eawt
An' th' emery paper an' a cleawt.

Then fotch a pail, an' yon owd plate
An' Ah'll scoop th'ash frae under t'grate."
Wi' t'sleeves rowelled up, deawn th'hoil hoo'd rooit
Amang o' th'ash, an' t'dust, an' t'sooit.

An' when hoo'd cleyned o' th'assoil eawt,
Hoo'd whiten th'hearthstooan reawnd abeawt,
Then blackleead t'grate az went ower th'hoil,
Ah'm capped hoo didn't blackleead t'coil!

Then o' reawnd th'oon, an' t'ribs an' t'shelf
Wur shone woll yo could see yerself,
Wi' th'emery paper reawnd a cleawt
Hoo'd rub t'top rib woll t'spots coom eawt.

Lang strakes deawn t'boiler could bi sin
Wheear t'watter'd dripped off t'ladin' tin.
Hoo rubbed an' polished woll hoo sweat
An' t'boiler front shone black as jet.

An' when hoo'd slekked o't'dust i't'reawm
Hoo'd cleyn o t'top o' t'fire-reawm.
When that wur done hoo'd say "Neaw lass,
Let's hev a do ut cleynin' t'brass!"

When t' "Tidy Betty" shone like gowd,
An' t'brass-railed fender---heaw we tow'd!
We'd lap 'em up to keep 'em cleean
Woll t'time to put 'em deawn ageean.

At t'weekend we'd put t'mattin' deawn
An' t'flag stooans reawnd we sceawred wi' breawn,
Wi' t'best rag rug fer under t'feet
We made yon room a gradely seet.

218

Az t'fireleet donced on t'new-cleyned brass
It sparkled like a bit o' glass,
An' t'cosiness inside eawr dooar
Wur worth o' t'wark we'd hed affooar.

Times change—an' neaw Ah've offen thowt
Machines does t'wark an' fooak does nowt!
Naht turn a knob or press a switch,
Yo've naht to know which switch is which!

Mi mother ud be capped to see
Heaw mich less wark thur is fer me.
But what Ah'd give to hear her sheawt
"Cum on, lass—get t'blackleead brush eawt!"

fire-arm	=	*mantleshelf*
naht	=	*local word for the more usual*
		'nobbut' (nought but)
woll	=	*whilst or while*
capped	=	*astonished*
cleawt	=	*cleaning-cloth*

THE COTTAGE OF
TIM BOBBIN IN MILNROW VILLAGE

Edwin Waugh (1817-1890)

THERE are some old people still living in Milnrow who were taught to read and write, and 'do sums' in Tim Bobbin's school, yet the majority of the inhabitants seem unacquainted with his real residence. I had myself been misled respecting it; but having obtained correct information and a reference from a friend in Rochdale to an old relative of his who lived in the veritable cottage of renowned Tim, I set about enquiring for him. As I entered the village, I met a sturdy good-looking woman, with a chocolate-coloured silk kerchief tied over her snowy cap, in that graceful way which is known over the countryside as the 'Mildro Bonnet'. She stopped me and said, "Meauster, hea fur han yo com'd?" "From Rochdale." "Han yo sin aught ov a felley wi breechuz on, un rayther forrud, oppo th'gate, between an th'Fir Grove?"

I told her I had not; and I then enquired of her for Scholefield that lived in Tim Bobbin's cottage. She reckoned up all the people she knew of that name; but none of them answering the description, I went on my way. I next asked a tall woollen weaver, who was striding up the street with his shuttle to the mending. Scratching his head, and looking thoughtfully round among the houses, he said, "Scwofil? Aw know no Scwofils, but thoose ut th' Tim Bobbin ale-heause; yodd'n bettur ask theer."

Stepping over to the Tim Bobbin inn, Mrs. Scholefield described to me the situation of Tim's cottage, near the bridge. Retracing my steps towards the place, I went into the house of an old acquaintance of my childhood. On the strength of a dim remembrance of my features, he invited me to sit down and share the meal just made ready for the family. "Come, poo a cheer up," said he, "an' need no moor laithein." After we had finished he said, "Neaw, win yo have a reech o' bacco? Mally, reytch us some chlyen pipes, an' t'pot eot o' t' nook. Let's see, hoo's lad are yo, sen yo; for aw welly forgetten, bith'mass." After a fruitless attempt at enlightening him thereon in ordinary town-English, I took to the dialect, and in the country fashion described my genealogy, on the mother's side. I was instantly comprehended; for he stopt me short with "Whau then, aw'll be sunken iv yo are not gron'son to Billy wi' th'pipes, at

220

th'Biggins'." "Yo han it neaw," said I, "Eh," replied he, "aw knowed him as weel as aw knew mi own feyther! He're a fyrfo chap for music an' sich like; an' he used to letter grave-stones an' do mason-work. Eh aw've bin to mony a orrytory wi' Owd Billy. Whau, let's see, Owd Wesley preytched at their heawse, i' Wardle fowd onc't. An' han yo some relations i' th' Mildro, then?" I told him my errand, and enquired for Scholefield, who lived in Tim Bobbin's cottage. As he pondered and turned the name over in his mind, one of his lads shouted out, "By th'mon, feyther, he mhyens 'Owd Mahogany'. Aw think he's code Scwofil, and he lives i' th'garden at th'bottom o' th'bonk, by th'wayter-side." It was generally agreed that this was the place, so I parted with my friends and went towards it. The old man came out without his hat, a short distance, to set me right. After bidding me a hearty "good neet", he turned round as he walked away and shouted out, "Neaw ta care yo coan th'next time yo com'n thiz gate, an' w'n have a gradely do!"

About twenty yards from the west end of the little stone bridge that spans the river, a lane leads between the ends of the dwelling houses down to the waterside. There, still sweetly secluded, stands the quaint, substantial cottage of John Collier, (Tim Bobbin) in its old garden by the edge of the Beal, which, flowing through the fields in front, towards the cottage, is there dammed up into a reservoir for the use of the mill close by, and then, tumbling over in a noisy little fall under the garden hedge, goes shouting and frolicking along the north-east side of it, over water-worn rocks, and under the bridge, till the cadence dies away in a low murmur beyond, where the bed of the stream gets smoother. Lifting the latch, I walked through the garden to the cottage where I found "Owd Mahogany" and his maiden sister, two plain, clean, substantial working people, who were sitting in the low-roofed, but otherwise roomy apartment in front, used as a kitchen. They entered heartily into the purpose of my visit, and showed me everything about the house with a genial pride. What made the matter more interesting was the fact that "Owd Mahogany" had been, when a lad, a pupil of Collier's. The house was built expressly for Tim, by his father-in-law; and the uncommon thickness of the walls, the number and arrangement of the rooms, and the remains of a fine old oak staircase, showed that more than usual care and expense had been bestowed upon it. As we went through the rooms on the ground floor, my ancient chaperone gave me a good deal of anecdote connected with each. Pointing to a clean, cold, whitewashed cell, with a great flag table in it, and a grid window at one end, he said "this wur his buttery, wheer he kept pullen, an gam, an sich like; for thir no mon i' Rachdaw parish livt betthur nor Owd Tim, nor moor like a gentleman; nor one at had moor friends, gentle an simple. Th'Teawnlo's took to him fyrfully, an thir'n olez othur comin' to see him, or sendin' him presents o' some mak'."

He next showed me the parlour where he (Tim Bobbin) used to write and receive company. A little oblong-room, low in the roof, and dimly lighted by a small window from the garden. Tim used to keep this retiring sanctum tastefully adorned with the flowers of each season, and one might have eaten their dinner off the floor in his time. In the garden he pointed out the corner where Tim had a roomy green arbor, with a smooth stone table in the middle, on which lay his books, his flute, or his meals, as he was in the mood. He would stretch himself out here, and muse for hours together. The lads used to bring their tasks from the school behind the house, to this arbor sometimes, for Tim to examine. He had a green shaded walk from the school into his garden. When in the school, or about the house, he wore a silk velvet skull cap. The famous radical, William Cobbett, used to wear a similar one occasionally; and I have heard those who have seen both in this trim, say that the likeness of the two men was then singularly striking.

"Owd Mahogany" having now shown and told me many interesting things respecting Tim's house and habits, entered into a hearty eulogy upon his character as a man and a schoolmaster. "He're a fine, straight forrad man, wi no maffle abeawt him, for o' his quare, cranky ways." As an author, he thought him: "Th' finest writer at Englan' bred at that time o'th'day." Of his caligraphy too, he seemed particularly proud, for he declared that: "Tim could write a clear print hond as smo as smithy smudge." He finished by saying that he saw him carried out of the doorway we were standing in, to his grave.

At the edge of the dark, I bade adieu to Tim's cottage and the comfortable old couple that live in it. As I looked back from the garden-gate, the house wore a plaintive aspect in my imagination, as if it was thinking of its fine old tenant.

MERSEYSIDE PUB

Joan Pomfret

All ports have pubs like these---
I find
In high Victorian rooms behind
The waterfront, an atmosphere
Of gas-light, dusty plush and beer.

Perhaps at night
When ships are in,
These mournful dark-brown walls begin
To live again, to smile and stare---
At mid-day only ghosts drink there.

Pale blondes sip port
And lemonade
With skippers of the China Trade,
And round the bar they bandy tales
Of tides and flying-fish and whales.

Cheroot smoke dims
The fly-blown gilt,
And hardy aspidistras wilt
As plump high-bosomed barmaids pass---
Time Please! . . And here's my empty glass.

THE YOUNG WITCH'S STORY

Miranda Roberts

I AM Jennet Device. Stay! Before you shun me and turn away in loathing, let me, I beg you, tell my story. . . If but to ease even after these years the burthen lying on my heart. I was nine years, remember, but nine years old when I was taken to give evidence against my mother, my grandmother, my sister Alizon and my brother James, known as an idiot. The judges were kind. . . I had known but little of kindness except perhaps from my father, John Device, whom old Chattox, to my knowledge, stared and bewitched to death. He provided her with an aghen or small sack of meal yearly; from fear, or other cause; and when through a wet harvest he could not give, she cursed him so that he fell sick unto death. "Jennet," he said to me often, "I am afeard of Chattox' eyes. She never takes them away from me, even though I lie here upstairs, and she be down below!"

He died, and died within me the last kindness. My grandmother, known as "old Demdike", was very proud of my evil looks, for I was even then ill-favoured, with odd-set eyes and matted fair locks. I was also small and stunted. Oh, how little my family realised, as they laughed at my ugly appearance, what hatred of them boiled in me! They would laugh and point, and call me "a real witch, a flaysome boggart in truth!" Silently I cursed them, and resolved to learn all I could about spells to curse them even better.

At first I was not allowed at the covens, but went just the same, hiding behind trees and in ditches, and seeing all the details of initiation and naming of familiars, and things even more horrible. I was so cunning that I was never found out, and kept on begging to be taken so that my mother consented— "if I could look on things without fear, and would swear never to reveal what I saw and heard." She would bewitch me to death, she said, if I ever said one word to a living soul. So I went and did not flinch or cry out, being by now used to such sights, and greatly enjoyed the stolen roast mutton, and bacon, cooked at a large open fire near our home, the Malkin Tower. I saw, absorbed and felt, and later told all to the examiners, who said I was bright and intelligent for one so young.

They seated me upon an oak table and asked me questions which I would not answer in the presence of my mother, who was looking at me with such dreadful eyes as chilled the blood, so she was removed, and I answered freely. My sister Alizon and my brother James also told of my mother's and grandmother's activities, such as cursing and bewitching people and animals, burying images, and waxen dolls stuck with pins. . . Boiling rats, frogs and owls, with scalps and teeth from the Newkirk graveyard; having in the house strange men in black long cloaks, their eyes covered by thick black masks; and hearing screams and shrieks in the night. Also I told of a large iron pot, deep and black, whose pale contents I could not put name to, and on whose surface floated a pinkish, noisome fat. . .

Well, I returned alone to the Malkin Tower. The others were taken away; to Lancaster I heard later. On reaching a lane near to our home I saw a woman who had visited us many times for herbs and potions made by my grandmother. She hurried past me, eyes averted, murmuring "Witch! . . . Murderer! . . . I thought I would be happy without the constant cruelties of my brother and sister, the sneers of my mother and grandmother, but I was afraid to stay alone at the Malkin. Men came, digging up the floor, searching the whole house, examining the very pots and pans. I was sent to a sister of my mother's, who promised to care for me. She lived in Burnley, so no more the wild, free wind off Pendle blowing over me, no more the sweet purple heather, the rough grass, the glad climb to the summit.

I scrubbed and toiled, and was cruelly used. "Your grandma is dead, and you have killed her," my aunt told me, three days after they had been removed to prison. Later---"Your mother, sister and brother are dead, and you are their murderer. ."

I looked at her with hate. She struck me across the mouth. That night I made a doll from clay, putting in her splay nose and tiny eyes, and her drawn-in upper lip. I stuck it with pins, and thrust it deep into the dying fire, uttering a curse I had often heard my mother use. She could not rise next day, but I neither fed nor gave her to drink, though she entreated me all night. I sat and stared at her, deep, deep into her eyes. Next day I gave her a brew of my own, she now so mad of thirst that she seized and drank it all off at one gulp. She died at midnight, rolling in agony and doubled in two. I ran for an old, almost blind doctor, saying that she had recently eaten a dish of mushrooms, and he gave me a certificate to that effect. I, being her only relative, claimed all her goods, which I sold, and, free, walked gladly back towards Pendle, finding a small cottage in the village of Newkirk.

There I stayed and lived much as my people had done, by supplying potions and simples to cure love and other ills; and if anyone looked askance or slighted me, I knew what to do, and soon was troubled no more. Years went by, yet I grew no more well-favoured but even uglier, and, at thirty, looked much older and a little bent. Yesterday I met old Jane Bulcock near to Pendle Water. Now past eighty, she is gnarled and twisted like an ancient bulloes tree. She was taken with my family to be examined at the Witch Trials, but found not guilty, though with my own eyes I have seen her do much evil.

"Witch-hunters are coming by again, thou'd better hide thyself. . .He-he-he!. . ."

I said: "Curses on thee, old dame, curses on thee. . . fall, fade and die, I command thee. . ."

She laughed evilly, but I made towards my home, I had heard rumours. Once more, all over again, the terror, the humiliations and agonies. I thought of those I had seen taken long ago. Their tormented eyes, without hope. . . nothing in sight but the rope---that, or the fire!

It grows dark; a while since, a sun of blood sank behind Pendle. From my cottage door I can see the chapel-of-rest, with God's Eye upon one wall. How sweet is the air, pure and cold; I will go in and light my dip, and have ale and ash-cakes. . . then to my bed.

I will not think of THEM; long, long ago they died. . . I did not mean to betray them, I was but nine years, I did not think, that day, that I should return alone to the Malkin Tower. The judges stroked my hair, spoke soft words. I am not used to such things, I felt warm and loved . . . and I told . . . I told!

I will live here by sweet Pendle, I will live and – who is there? Who is there in the shadows? Go away. . . go away. . . I did not kill her, she ate mushrooms! . . .Nor did I mean THEM to die. . . I could not love them, but they were there, with me; go away. . . do not come hear. . . loose me, curses on you. . . fall and fade and die. . .I command you. . .Oh, Lord, save me. . .have mercy on me, help me, I pray thee. . .

(*Jennet Device, or Davies was re-arrested in 1633, but was again released through lack of evidence, as were all the ones who were arrested with her.*)

AH'VE STARTED A-COURTIN' AGEN

Clifford Heyworth (Bill o'Bow's)

This world is a place full o' trouble an' care,
A've oft bin o'erladened misel wi' despair,
But neaw Aw'm as happy an' blithe as a lark,
For neet time's no longer aw empty an' dark;
　　For agen, for agen,
Aw've started a-courtin' agen.

Th'first lassie Aw met, well aw thowt hoo wer' fine,
Aw warked an' Aw slaved that one day hoo'd be mine,
Aw bowt her a ring, but then, oh, dear-a-me,
Hoo flitted an' went to live eawt bi t'blue sea.
　　Once agen, once agen,
Mi courtin' wer' done through yon post-box, agen.

Aw went o'er to pay her a visit one June,
Her mother said — "Eh, lad, tha's come o'er too soon,
For next week at this time, a weddin' there'll be,
An' t'lass ut tha claims, ull be t'bride, dosta see?"
　　Theer agen — theer agen,
Aw wer' no longer claimin' a lass for misen.

That day when Aw met her Aw felt such a foo',
Hoo said — "Meet mi Charlie," — said Aw — "How d'yo do,"
Aw couldna stand t'strain o' that terrible blow,
It shook me fro' t'creawn o' mi yed to mi toe.
　　For agen — for agen,
Aw wer' no longer courtin' a-courtin' agen.

But owd "Doctor Time" gradely treated mi wound,
He cured mi depression an' made me feel sound,
His 'physic' warked wonders an' made mi feel wick,
Mi heart soon contracted love's germ in a tick,
　　Once agen — once agen
Aw'd started a-courtin' a lass, once agen.

One mornin', when singin' wi' voice full o' glee,
Mi mother said — "Neaw lad, what's comin' o'er thee?
Aw've noticed th'art shavin' thisel every day. . ."
Said Aw — "Listen, mother, Aw'm reight preawd to say —
    That agen — that agen
Aw've started a-courtin', it's true! Once agen!"

When t'weather is stormy, t'sun shines on me still,
Aw sing as Aw wark, and Aw wark wi' a will.
Ther's never no shadows fro' cleawds up aboon,
It's summer year reawnd, for December's like June.
    Neaw agen — neaw agen
Aw've started a-courtin' a-courtin' agen.

Wi' her Aw shall settle, o' that Aw've no fear,
For last neet ut sale-room, we bowt an armchear;
In her bottom drawer — well, ther's mony a thing,
An' soon on her finger hoo'll wear a gowd ring.
    'Cause agen — 'cause agen —
Aw've started a-courtin' a-courtin' agen.

An' when we have travelled a long way in ye'rs,
Mi earthly possessions will also be hers,
Together we'll sit by eawr own fireside,
An' talk o'er that day when hoo wer' mi sweet bride,
    An' agen — an' agen —
We'll *both* do eawr courtin' agen an' agen.

BLACK AN' WHITE

Harvey Kershaw

SOMEBODY once said; "Never shake a bridle o'er a Yorkshireman's grave, or he'll get up an' pinch thi horse!" Maybe that's why Ted Oakroyd were so tight-fisted, an' wouldn't part wi' t'skin off his porritch. Ted were an "off-coomed" un fro' Yorkshire, who'd coom o'er to t' gradely side o' t'Pennines to wed a Lancashire lass an' mak' hisel' awhom theer. He'd ne'er tak' onnybody's word for owt, till he'd seen it wi' his own e'en, printed i' t'papper, i' black an' white.

A real Yorkshireman, Ted ne'er did nowt for nowt, for onnybody except hisel'; he were allus on t'mak', an' there were nowt 'at he liked more nor brass. Besides warkin' at t'mill as a weyver, he sowd pot-yarbs an' plants an' o' maks o' vegetables, 'at he grew in his little cottage garden. Then he geet a dozen hens an' a bantam-cock, an' hauve a dozen ducks, so's he could addle more brass wi' sellin' eggs.

If onnybody wanted to buy aught off him durin' t'middle o' t'week, an' couldn't pay him till pay-day, he allus made 'em sign an I.O.U., for there were nowt, he said, like havin' it i'black an' white. He geet tekken deawn a peg one neet, heawever, an' larnt 'at things weren't allus o'reet, e'en when he'd getten things i' black and white.

Caleb Ramshaw an' Jonty Sykes were two owd cronies who were gam for a marlock onny time. One neet while sittin' i' t' "Ring o' Bells" they geet their yeds together, an' decided to teych Ted Oakroyd a lesson. They knew 'at Ted would be comin' to t' "Ring o' Bells" that neet, fotchin' eggs an' stuff for t'londlort's missus; smokin' quietly i' th'ingle-nook, they kept a close watch through t'window, an' tarried till Ted were spotted coomin' deawn t'road.

Then, as Ted were makkin' for t'front dur, Jonty piked eawt o't'back dur, an' made his way to t'village pond, wheer Ted's ducks were swimmin' areawnd. 'Twer welly th'edge o' dark, an' rainin' heavily, so there wern't a wick soal to be seen – quickly Jonty managed to get howd o' two o't' ducks, then, wi' some black soot 'at he'd browt wi' him, he daubed each bird till they were o' black an' white spots.

While this were gooin' on, Ted had getten rid of his eggs an' things at t' "Ring o' Bells", an' as he were abeawt to goo, Caleb collared him an' axed him heaw his ducks were gettin' on.

"Champion" replied Ted. "Aw nobbut wish 'at Aw'd getten three times as monny."

"Why, heaw's that?" axed Caleb, fausely.

"Well, tha knows, folk look forrard to havin' a bit o' roast duck wi' t'season's first crop o' peighs," Ted explained. "An' t' more ducks Aw have then, an' more ducks Aw con sell. They's fotch me a bonny bit o' brass, to help me along."

Just then Jonty burst in t'room, wi' a squawkin' duck wrigglin' 'neath each arm.

"Th'art just th'felly Aw want to see!" said Jonty, puffin' to get his wynt back.

Ted looked flabbergasted, an' axed: "What dost want wi' me?"

"Aw've feawnd these two ducks strayin' o'er th'hill yonder. Nobody seems to own 'em, tha con ha' both of 'em for a hauve-sovereign." Jonty towd him.

Ted looked at th'ducks an' said: "They're noan o' mine shuzheaw. My lot's o' white, them are o' black an' white dots. Onnyroad, Aw'll gi' thi three hauve-creawns for 'em, what dost say?"

"Let's be seein' t'colour o' thi brass, then tha con tak 'em," agreed Jonty, winkin' slyly at Caleb.

Ted stumped up, grudgin'ly, then geet owd of a duck wi' each arm an' ambled off to'ards whom. Eawtside, he geet copped i' a rain-storm, an' bi' t' time he'd getten whom he were soaked to t'skin, an' witcherd. But awhom he feawnd 'at t'rain had done summat more nor drench him, for when he looked at t'ducks i' his arms, he saw 'at t'wavter. runnin' off each duck's back, had weyshed o' t'black spots away.

Rushin' reawnd to t'duck cote, he ceawnted up an' feawnd 'at he were two ducks missin', then he twigged what had happened. He set off back to t' "Ring o' Bells" as fast as his bow-legs 'd carry him, an' theer, lookin' so meek an' mild, were Caleb an' Jonty.

"Hello, owd fettler, th'art back soon, what's amiss?" axed Caleb.

"Tha knows full weel what's up – tha's sowd me two o' mi own ducks – give us mi brass back afore Aw fotch t'bobby!" fumed Ted.

"Nay, that's noan reet," said Jonty. "Tha towd us they weren't thine, as *thy* ducks were o' white 'uns."

"So were them 'at yo sowd mi, afore yo meddled wi' 'em!" spluttered Ted.

"Look thi here, Ted," Caleb chimed in. "Tha's allus said 'at nowt's reet if tha doesn't see it i' black an' white — weel then, tha connut grumble, tha geet thi ducks i' black an' white, didn't tha?"

Ted's face, 'at looked as black as thunder when he yerd this, t'next minute turned white at t'gills as Caleb honded him his three hauve-creawns, an' said: "Here tha art, tak howd o' this, an' remember "A foo' is soon parted fro' his brass!"

Pocketin' t'brass, Ted, peeved at havin' been 'bested', were just stalkin' off whom agen, when Caleb an' Jonty co'ed after him: "Next time tha goos o'er to Yorkshire an' tha meets thi cricketin' pals, dunnot forget to tell 'em 'at two Lancashire lads caught thi eawt wi' two ducks i' one neet!"

CONCLUSION

Well, now we've met and had our 'crack'
With many a tale and song
And memory of the two great Shires
Where all of us belong.

And if in passing it appears
We've thought the same, and said —
That's only what's expected of
The White Rose and the Red!

The oak, the ash, the ivy tree,
The North wind and the rain
Nurtured us both — no wonder that
We sing the same refrain.

No wonder that we feel the bond
Between us will abide,
And hope you, too, enjoyed our songs
And laughed with us, and cried!
So now may 'Tykes' and 'Tacklers' both
Whole-heartedly agree
That our exchange of views has sealed
This bond 'TWIXT THEE AND ME'.